THE PO

MW00414761

WILDERNESS
SURVIVAL KIT

THE POOR MAN'S
WILDERNESS
SURVIVAL KIT

ASSEMBLING YOUR EMERGENCY
GEAR FOR LITTLE OR NO MONEY

James Ballou

Paladin Press • Boulder, Colorado

Other books by James Ballou:
Arming for the Apocalypse
Long-Term Survival in the Coming Dark Age
Makeshift Workshop Skills for Survival and Self-Reliance
More Makeshift Workshop Skills

The Poor Man's Wilderness Survival Kit:
Assembling Your Emergency Gear for Little or No Money
by James Ballou

Copyright © 2013 by James Ballou

ISBN 13: 978-1-61004-860-6
Printed in the United States of America

Published by Paladin Press, a division of
Paladin Enterprises, Inc.,
P.O. Box 1307
Boulder, Colorado 80306 USA
+1.303.443.7250

Direct inquiries and/or orders to the above address.

Visit our website at www.paladin-press.com.

CONTENTS

WARNING

The information in this book is based on the experiences, research, and beliefs of the author and cannot be duplicated exactly by readers. The author, publisher, and distributors of this book disclaim any liability from any damage or injury of any type that a reader or user of information contained in this book may incur from the use or misuse of said information. This book is *for academic study only.*

INTRODUCTION

The purpose of this book is to offer the reader a variety of ideas to create or acquire wilderness survival gear on a strictly limited budget, then organize the pertinent gear into self-contained, portable, emergency survival kits. Readers will certainly find no shortage of books and websites these days that provide comprehensive information about survival kits, bug-out bags, and all the latest and best outdoor gear, but throughout this book we will explore the prospect of assembling usable wilderness survival kits at very little cost, or in some instances with no money investment at all.

I believe this is a legitimate and very useful focus for a survival book in our present economy, where so many people are unemployed, losing their homes to foreclosure, having to pay more than $3 per gallon for gasoline, and simply struggling to make ends meet. Regardless of the financial stresses, outdoor survival gear will always be important for hikers, hunters, campers, firewood gatherers, homeless nomads, or other wilderness adventurers, because the right equipment could be a contributing factor affecting an individual's well-being in the elements.

Basic survival kit items displayed in several of the fundamental survival requirement categories. No single item in this photo cost more than $2, and that wooden whistle, which is very loud, was homemade.

Even those who can afford to assemble an elaborate survival kit consisting of the latest and most expensive components may wish to assemble a few additional kits for backup survival caches. Those extra kits ideally will consist mainly of low-budget supplies, because as strictly backup systems they will most likely not be needed.

Ready-made kits are available from numerous sources, but they can be costly and their scope is very generic. Because survival requirements can be different from one person to another, it seems logical to customize your survival or outdoor kit to address your own unique priorities. A kit for someone living in southern Alabama will differ from one intended for use in northern Minnesota. Hunters in the fall season would have different weather concerns than summer campers or winter cross-country skiers. A knife and a shoelace could be lifesaving tools to the guy who knows how to build and use a bow drill for making fire but totally useless to someone without the necessary skills.

Assembling a personalized, comprehensive wilderness survival kit with the highest quality or the latest, most innovative, or most efficient products available can easily add up to well over several hundred dollars, and I know an awful lot of people who would not easily be able to afford that kind of an investment. Fortunately, we do not have to spend big bucks to accomplish the basic task.

There undoubtedly will be those who read this book and wonder why anyone would willingly opt for inferior or makeshift "poor man's" gear to trust his life on while clearly superior equipment is available. And I think that's a valid question to ask. Readers might wonder if, with this book, I am advocating always going cheap. I would answer that with a "no"—at least not advocating always going cheap for *everyone*. If you can afford the best outdoor gear on the market, by all means get it!

What I am mainly trying to achieve with this book is to illustrate some workable ideas for those who may be forced to operate within a narrow budget and provide some hopefully intriguing and entertaining tidbits in the process. And even if you do happen to have the resources and end up acquiring all the latest and best gear, there are no guarantees that you would actually have that equipment with you when an emergency survival scenario occurs. You might have to assemble your adventure kit in a place and time not of your choosing, for whatever unforeseen reason, with whatever you find available then. So the distinction I would stress here is that the equipment described in this book would not necessarily constitute my *first choice* items. They are merely additional possibilities.

So this book is really about exploring as many alternatives to the more conventional gear as its scope will allow and introduce you to a variety of intriguing ideas on the subject. I hope it will inspire you to devise your own great wilderness kits and assemble them as economically as possible.

CHAPTER ONE

POOR MAN'S KIT CONTAINER

Regardless of what size we aim to build our kit or the specific purposes we want it to address, it makes sense to start with what to pack it in. Every type of kit—be it a first-aid kit, a field shaving kit, a gun-cleaning kit, or a wilderness survival kit like we are talking about here—needs to be housed in some type of container to keep its components together and secure.

Small, pocket-sized kits have been packed by wilderness travelers in such containers as belt pouches; those old metal Band-Aid cans; tough plastic waterproof boxes; and even compact tobacco tins, spice tins, tea canisters, and Altoids mint tins. Larger kits are commonly housed in shoulder bags, duffel bags, fanny packs, or backpacks.

In my view, the most important criteria for the kit container should be that it serves to securely retain and protect the important contents in the most conveniently portable way possible. For this discussion, our chosen container should also be obtainable at little or no cost.

Some examples of survival kit containers for small- to medium-sized kits, including a nylon cloth belt pouch, an aluminum box with locking lid, Altoids mints tin, small metal coffee can, metal spice canister, metal Band-Aid box, cat food can with plastic lid, small plastic first-aid kit box, and a plastic bottle with screw-on lid. Of these, the belt pouch at $12 was the most expensive.

Either a daypack or a canvas bag, commonly found on the cheap at second-hand sales, will serve as a conveniently portable kit container for a medium-large survival kit.

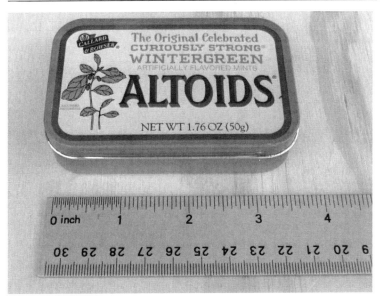

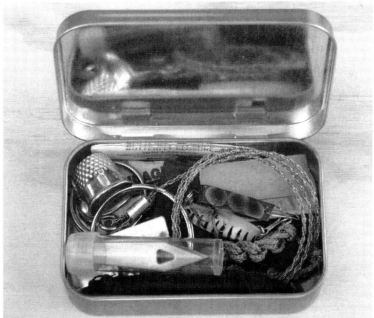

An Altoids mints box can be a convenient container for a very small pocket outdoor survival kit because it is relatively small and flat.

DEFINING THE APPLICATION REQUIREMENTS FOR THE KIT

The first variable you should define before settling upon one type of container or another is the anticipated scope of your individual kit's application, which will help you decide on the size parameters for the completed kit.

For example, if its intended purpose is merely to help us survive a night or two in the woods and get a fire going in winter conditions, maybe build a few wire snares to trap small animals, catch a few fish

This little canvas zippered pouch will slide onto a belt and securely house half a pound of small survival gear.

from a mountain stream, and signal to rescuers, then we might have confidence in a very basic and compact kit that would fit inside a coat pocket, perhaps housed within something like an Altoids tin.

If, on the other hand, you expect to survive a month or two in the remote bush of Alaska or the vast Amazon jungle before returning to civilization, then you will likely assemble something more than just a pocket kit—maybe something like a backpack loaded with essential outdoor gear appropriate for the particular climate and dangers, and of a sufficient amount to support your survival for that duration. So, answering the question as to what you expect from your individual kit will tell you basically how large or small you should make it and what should go in it. At that point, you will be ready to search for the perfect container.

The other primary concern is cost. We want the best container at the lowest possible investment. That means we will have to scrounge around at flea markets, thrift stores, garage sales, or around our house until we find exactly what will serve our purpose.

You may have to get creative and resourceful in your

This Altoids tin survival kit is tightly wrapped with cord to keep it closed—and to have some extra, vital cordage on hand.

search. You could begin by searching around the house for something you might already have that could be made to serve. If you take a close look at some routinely discarded containers, you just might find exactly what you want, and you will have acquired it for free merely by rescuing it from the trash bin.

METAL CONTAINERS

When I was growing up, the conventional Band-Aid container from the Johnson & Johnson Company was a neat little metal box with a hinged lid. I would save these containers for my basic fishing tackle or other small items, and I always considered them to be a perfectly handy size for my compact outdoor gear. I would usually wrap a rubber band around the box to keep its hinged lid from flopping open. These metal tins also have shiny surfaces on their bottoms and inside their lids that could serve as expedient mirrors for signaling.

The common metal coffee can with its convenient plastic lid is a popular survival kit container that I believe has merit,

The bandage tin will conveniently house the small survival gear basics.

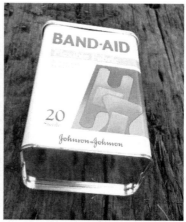

The shiny bottom of the tin could also serve as a signal mirror in an emergency.

The 11-oz. metal coffee can has potential for service as an economical medium-size survival kit container. The outside of this one has been wrapped with duct tape and cord to increase its versatility.

because even the smallest regular size—11-ounce net volume that measures approximately 4 inches in diameter and 5½ inches in height—will hold an impressive amount of small survival gear. And this is a container that is routinely discarded and readily obtainable for free.

In addition to serving as our main survival kit container, the can itself could be used as a cooking vessel, candle lantern, water pail, wash basin, dipping ladle, drinking mug, makeshift stove, or just a spool for duct tape or cord. Tie or tape a small strap or length of rope to the outside to make the unit easier to carry on a belt or suspend from the wall frame or ceiling inside your survival shelter or tent.

TINY KIT CONTAINERS

Within the main kit, you will find uses for other smaller containers to keep certain items separated or protected from the rest of the gear.

Small containers suitable for keeping things like stick matches or sewing needles are easily fabricated from ink pen bodies or empty rifle or shotgun shell cases. Very little, if any,

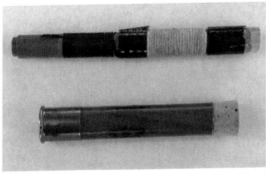

Above: Sewing needle cases improvised from an ink pen body at top and a trimmed empty .410 shotgun shell at bottom, both capped at their open ends with small cork stoppers.

Right: This empty 12-gauge shot shell capped with a cork will hold fishhooks, artificial flies, matches, thread, dental floss, safety pins, a P-38 can opener, and several tiny hobby knife blades.

preparation is needed with brass rifle casings, other than maybe cleaning out the inside before finding the appropriately sized cork stopper and then adding the contents.

The crimped openings of spent shotgun shells usually do need to be trimmed up evenly with a sharp knife. Cap the openings with small cork stoppers or tapered wooden plugs; even a little strip of duct tape can serve as a sticky flap to cover the opening. If you are creating an expedient needle

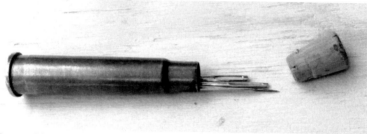

Empty .303 British brass cartridge serves as an expedient needle case.

The needle case closed with a cork stopper.

A spent 16-gauge shotgun shell serves as a container for matches, fishhooks, sewing needles, and more. Note that the outside is wrapped with thread in order to keep a supply with the kit.

case, wrap the outside of the shell with sewing thread so that the item conveniently serves as both a container *and* a spool. If there is any worry that the cork will work itself out loose while riding in the kit, wrap a small strip of tape around the cork to hold it in place until needed.

Very small containers can be improvised in a variety of other ways. You can envelope the tiniest items—such as fishhooks, split shot sinkers, fishing lures, wooden matches,

aspirin tablets, safety pins, and tiny gun screws—inside a folded piece of heavy paper or cardboard and then wrap the outside with aluminum foil to hold everything securely together. This type of makeshift packaging would at least prevent the tiny items from loosely mixing in with all the other gear within the kit.

A MESS KIT FOR OUR SURVIVAL KIT CONTAINER

Another practical method for housing a

Above: We might as well use that space inside of our mess kit for storage of the essential wilderness survival gear.

Right: The aluminum mess kit closed and secure for stowing in the pack.

medium-size wilderness survival kit is to pack all the items into a backpacker's aluminum or stainless-steel mess kit pot that has its own pan-shaped lid with some type of folding handle that typically locks everything together. This is a very secure system because it's a sturdy metal container, and since the mess kit will probably go inside the pack anyway, being the valuable piece of outdoor equipment that it is, you might as well use all of that space inside for something. Most of these mess kits are not watertight, but you can achieve makeshift waterproofing by sealing one inside a gallon-sized zip-lock bag. This trick works with the classic smaller mess kits, but it won't for the larger, modern kits on the market.

THE SURVIVAL VEST

A suitable carry system for a medium-size survival kit is a vest with pockets that can be filled with gear and comfortably worn on the upper body like a jacket. These vests are popular

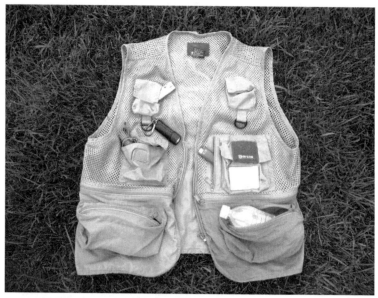

This fishing vest, with all of its pockets and pouches, provides a convenient way to carry a considerable amount of small survival gear.

with fishermen, photographers, reporters, and anyone who needs to carry lots of small items in the field. I was given a used and well-worn fishing vest that contains an assortment of pockets and pouches that is ideally suited to serve as an emergency survival vest.

THE WALLET SURVIVAL KIT

A seemingly unlikely holder for an ultracompact survival kit is a common trifold man's wallet. While a wallet may not be a viable container system for bulky things like flashlights or emergency blankets, and it won't be the most secure container system you could ever find, it could nevertheless hold a surprising amount of very small or flat items, including a signal mirror, square of aluminum foil, small-diameter cord or dental floss, fishhooks, small blades, matches, sewing gear, paper survival or first-aid instructions, and other tiny but useful items for the woods. The best thing about it is that it

Using a trifold wallet as a convenient holder for small survival gear.

will comfortably fit into most jacket and pants pockets or in a vehicle glove box. Assemble two such wallets and you'd be surprised how well equipped you might find yourself.

SURVIVAL KIT IN A BAG

One of the cheapest kit containers I can think of is merely a zip-seal plastic bag (such as those from Ziploc) that can be zipped shut to hold the contents in and keep water out. The freezer bags are thicker and more durable than the standard clear zipper bags. Besides its low cost, another advantage to a zip-lock plastic bag over other containers is that it is easy to see what is inside and where everything is positioned without having to open the container. The biggest disadvantage to the bag is that it is softer than any of the metal or hard plastic containers and therefore should not be trusted to protect the contents as well. My recommendation would be to use at least two bags, one inside the other, for double thickness protection.

Survival kit items carried in a clear plastic Ziploc bag.

FOOD STORAGE CONTAINERS FOR SURVIVAL KITS

Perhaps one of the most practical containers for small survival kits is one of the common plastic food storage containers that are so popular these days, especially the tough, thick, clear plastic variety with lid latches and rubber seal rings that keep them airtight. These containers are rugged, waterproof, and lightweight; most of them have enough volume capacity to house a healthy supply of small survival gear; and they provide excellent protection for their contents. They are transparent, so you can see what is inside, and the best thing for our purposes is that they are not prohibitively expensive.

SURVIVAL KIT PACKS

Backpacks and fanny packs obviously are excellent systems for carrying all sorts of gear. If you want to assemble a kit large enough for a long-term self-sufficient wilderness situation, then a pack system of some sort is hard to beat.

Typical plastic food container. Lightweight, durable, transparent, waterproof, and inexpensive.

A "jumbo-sized" fanny pack, such as the author's long-range outfit shown here, will easily hold 30 pounds of outdoor gear. Note the modified U.S. Army LBE shoulder strap suspenders added to help manage the load.

There are any number of expensive packs available for serious long-range hikers, but we can still outfit ourselves quite well along these lines on very little money. Over the years, I have encountered more hiker backpacks at yard sales than I could count, and most of them ranged between $2 and $10 apiece. In fact, for a while I was collecting them until I eventually ran out of space to store them!

An even more economical alternative is the famous backpack adapted from an old pair of jeans, sometimes referred to as a "pants pack." I first read about this idea around ten years ago in a magazine article written by the resourceful survival instructor and author Christopher Nyerges. What makes the idea so great is that it is ridiculously quick and easy to create, uses an item that almost everyone already has on hand, and doesn't permanently alter the pants in any way. When you're done with the pack, simply untie the cords and return the jeans to service as clothing!

The load-carrying capacity of the pants pack will depend to a large degree on the strength of the belt loop attach

Assorted packs and pack frames from yard sales. No single item in this photo cost more than $5.

The pant legs are tied to the belt loops with cord to create shoulder straps, and a rope is used as a belt to cinch the top closed.

Demonstrating the pants pack.

points, which could always be reinforced if needed.

Fanny packs are considerably smaller than conventional full-sized backpacks, but one of the large sizes of fanny packs will hold quite a lot of field gear. Wrap some outdoor clothing (e.g., wool sweater, raingear) in a heavy-duty plastic bag and lash it to the top of a fanny pack and you will have the same amount of survival gear on you as you would with a typical day-hike backpack.

In this photo we see an example of a fanny pack kit that is commonly carried by the author on day hikes into the woods. It includes a metal cup, knitted wool gloves, small pliers, lock-blade knife, plastic hand trowel, assorted bits of cordage, fishing tackle in a small plastic bottle, insect repellent, cotton rag, fire-making supplies, and miscellaneous small tools. This is a very convenient carry system for a medium to large survival kit.

CHAPTER TWO

POOR MAN'S
EDGED TOOLS

There are certain fundamental pieces of survival gear that belong in every size of kit, and we can identify these by focusing on the most essential survival requirements. For example, we all know that at least three basic requirements of human existence are food, water, and shelter. Equipment that can help provide us with any of these three necessities warrants our consideration for inclusion in our kit, perhaps ahead of other useful gear.

Knives and hatchets are arguably the most fundamental tools for general use in the wilderness. Without them, it is awfully difficult or next to impossible to accomplish such basic tasks as cutting rope or other cord, cutting and sharpening stakes or poles for shelters, or skinning and butchering animals. So you can see how a blade can be helpful with two basic survival requirements in this example alone—food and shelter.

At the same time, it is usually not necessary to use the most expensive tools for these tasks. Under the majority of likely survival circumstances, you could get by quite well with edged tools that don't cost an arm and a leg. What you ultimately decide to be the best survival-kit tool for your money will depend on several factors.

This imported but very usable lock-blade folding knife is sold at the Wal-Mart store in my town under the brand name Ozark Trail for the retail price of just $1!

You have to face the issue of size right off the bat, because the knife or other edged tool must fit into whatever size kit you are assembling. There are many excellent folding knives on the market today that are very compact, but not all of them are "poor man cheap." To stay within strict budgetary restraints, you have to force yourself to think outside of the proverbial box.

THE YARD SALE SPECIAL

Just as is true with used packs and other useful second-hand wilderness equipment, a typically fruitful source of usable tools at low prices is the local garage sale. Those of us who routinely shop at these sales—call them garage sales, yard sales, moving sales, rummage sales, or whatever you want—eventually encounter countless inexpensive knives. The quality and condition will range anywhere from excellent to barely usable, so a shopper needs to be discriminating.

In addition to the typical neighborhood garage sale, the local flea market, with its flock of vendors peddling their antiques, military surplus, imported tools, and other odd "junk," is another excellent marketplace for used and reasonably priced knives.

TINY, INEXPENSIVE BLADES SUITABLE AS SURVIVAL KNIVES

Small, sharp, stainless-steel replacement blades for X-Acto knives and other brand hobby tools, box cutter/single-edged razor blades, and retractable drywall/utility knife blades are sold in every hardware store and are not at all expensive. These blades have the advantage of being able to fit into almost any size kit because they are so small and light. But their size also limits their utility to a degree because they simply cannot perform certain heavy-duty tasks in the field as well as the larger edged tools can, like chopping thick tree branches or quickly gutting and skinning game, so they might be viewed strictly as backup tools to our larger knives.

Nevertheless, the tiniest and thinnest sharp blades can be very useful for many of the numerous light-duty tasks a survivor is likely to encounter in the wilderness, such as carving wood, boring small holes or cutting thin notches in tree branches, gutting fish, sewing torn clothing or shelter material,

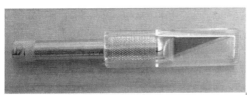

Above: This $3 hobby knife wears a plastic point protector, and its aluminum handle has been shortened to make it more compact for stowing in a small survival kit.

Right: Small blades ideal for compact survival kits, from top: single-edged razor/window scraper blade, hobby knife blade, and drywall knife replacement blade.

The little hobby knife blade becomes instantly more usable with a dowel or stick firmly attached for a handle.

The sharp edge of a single-edged razor blade is protected in a partially slit cork. A great way to store this blade without damaging its blade or the other gear in your kit—and in a pinch, the cork can be used as a fire starter or fishing bobber.

Razor blades also have more utility when attached to sticks or other makeshift handles.

severing string and twine, shaving facial whiskers, or even performing emergency surgery. You can attach a makeshift handle in the field to enhance the handling characteristics and general capabilities of the blade.

Comfortable handles could also be devised for these tiny blades well before any survival emergency. A short piece of hardwood dowel is very easy to shape and attach to any of these little blades and at a negligible cost, using common hand tools the average homeowner already has on hand. If

Utility blade attached to a convenient makeshift wooden handle.

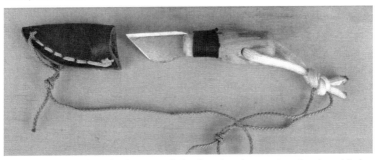

The same little knife with a homemade leather sheath to protect the sharp blade.

designed properly, this survival cutting tool will not be too bulky for the kit. A utility knife blade (package of five blades purchased at the local hardware store for just under $2) can also be shaped using a bench grinder to accommodate whatever style and size of handle you want.

SURVIVAL KNIVES FROM KITCHEN KNIVES

I don't think we should overlook the common butcher knife or general-duty kitchen knife when gearing up for survival. These tools are utility oriented, widely available, and very inexpensive, especially when purchased used. Kitchen knives of all varieties tend to be a dime a dozen at thrift stores and yard sales. Most of them will be dull and will require special attention to hone their edges, but that is a minor issue that is easily corrected. Knives with serrated edges, while difficult or in some instances impractical for resharpening, still have merits when it comes to certain tasks in the field, like slicing through cord or harvesting pine boughs for bedding.

Most of the inexpensive kitchen knives you encounter will lack blade covers, but you will want something to protect their sharp edges in the field. You can improvise your own expedient but functional blade covering or sheath out of heavy cardboard and duct tape if you lack scraps of cowhide or other material with which to build a better sheath. The biggest drawback to the cardboard and tape sheath is that it won't handle moisture very well, and that could be a major drawback in an outdoor environment. I would not expect it to last as long or hold up as well as a leather or plastic sheath under heavy usage. Even so, my own experimental cardboard and duct tape blade covers have served my purposes well as temporary expedients.

I also look for the heaviest, thickest blades I can find because so many of the knives intended for kitchen applications have comparatively thin blades. You want as much durability in your survival tools as possible.

Low-cost, secondhand kitchen knives, from left: customized old Forgecraft carbon kitchen knife with leather sheath, stainless-steel butcher knife with cardboard and duct tape sheath, and a common serrated steak knife. Any of these "thrift store specials" will cut, carve, and chop when called upon to serve you, even in a wilderness survival situation.

Perhaps the biggest downside to the common low-cost kitchen knife is that it is not normally compact, so it probably won't fit into our smallest survival kits. In some instances, it might be practical to shorten the length of the blade. One option is to cut off the tip end along the desired line using a disk grinder or a rotary tool like a Dremel Tool, then reshape the blade on a bench grinder and sharpen as needed for a custom-sized survival knife.

EXPEDIENT HOMEMADE SURVIVAL KNIVES

Finally, you can build your own low-cost edged tools so they are custom-tailored to your individual survival kit. Just about any small, flat piece of steel can be shaped into a functional knife blade using either a grinding wheel; a hacksaw and file; or, with enormous amounts of sweat and perseverance, a large abrasive rock with a relatively flat surface (or alternatively the surface of a brick if available) to abrade the steel to the desired cutting edge. The resulting tool doesn't have to be pretty or perfect, just sharp and functional.

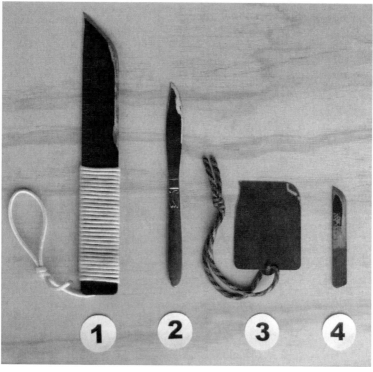

Improvised edged tools: 1) camp knife ground from a section of an old, rusty carpenter's square, its handle area wrapped with parachute cord, 2) stainless-steel butter knife sharpened to serve as a general-purpose cutting tool, 3) hiker's signal mirror sharpened into a cutting tool, and 4) small survival kit knife ground from a small flat bastard file.

Several commonly available items that come to mind for modification into an expedient cutting edge for survival include an inexpensive steel pocket signal mirror that is very thin and easy to grind a sharp cutting edge on; a butter knife; a broken or well-worn small flat bastard file; an old, worn saw blade; a lawn mower or edger blade; a strap hinge; a garden trowel; or just about any flat piece of junk steel you might find around the house or shop.

Many of the steel products commonly available for making improvised blades will be of relatively soft, low-carbon or mild steel, and this material will not produce or hold an edge nearly as well as will much harder steel. But in a pinch, our makeshift knife from mild steel could still be made to cut, chop, pry, dig, stab, or scrape as needed in a wilderness survival situation. It is also easier to quickly sharpen a rough but functional edge on mild steel with just a few swipes of a bastard file than it is to hone a finer edge on a hard steel blade.

SCISSORS FOR THE SURVIVAL KIT

One of the handiest edged tools around camp is a common pair of sharp, sturdy steel scissors. With scissors (shears), a woodsman can quickly and cleanly cut lengths of twine or small-diameter rope like parachute cord or bootlaces for endless purposes, trim fraying edges of canvas, perform haircuts, trim fingernails and toenails, cleanly open plastic or foil food packaging using only one hand, snip through fishing line, and accomplish numerous tasks in clothing repair or leatherwork. It is true that many of these tasks could also be accomplished using the blade of a sharp knife, but for so many applications, the scissors are simply more practical and easier to use.

Used scissors in good condition are very easy to find at bargain prices. On more than one occasion, I have found quality brand stainless-steel scissors, used but in excellent condition, at yard sales for no more than a dollar a pair, and that is indeed a lot of tool for the money.

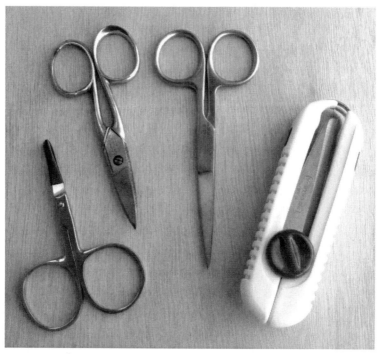

Stainless-steel scissors, especially the smallest sizes or the sturdiest folding models, will be easy to pack into a medium-size survival kit and will be well worth their weight.

The blades of small scissors protected within a homemade leather sheath.

You will probably want quality stainless scissors in the smaller sizes to fit your survival kits, even though they won't provide as much leverage for heavy cutting as do the largest pairs. Also, a sheath or blade cover will keep the blades closed in the kit and help protect them. A blade cover for scissors is usually much easier to fabricate than a regular knife sheath because all it has to do is keep the scissor blades closed. You can sandwich the blades between two strips of cowhide and stitch their outer edges together. For the less ambitious, bend a piece of cardboard around the scissors and wrap the "sheath" shut with duct tape, or simply keep the scissors closed with a couple twists of wire.

CHAPTER THREE

POOR MAN'S WATER CONTAINERS

Besides having functional knives and tools, having some way to collect, carry, and treat water could possibly be the most important concern for anyone traveling into the wild places. Without water to drink, no person can expect to survive very long at all.

WATER CONTAINERS

A variety of primitive water containers were used successfully for thousands of years, including fired and waterproof clay vessels, wooden vessels, hollowed gourds, animal horns, and even water bags made from animal intestines and skins.

We have many more wonderfully practical and often ridiculously inexpensive options available to us now. Many of the disposable plastic bottles that drinks come in are already ideal vessels just the way they are for keeping liquids, and we can employ them with our regular outdoor survival gear at almost no cost whatsoever. And don't overlook the obvious: plastic water bottles are given out for free as promotional items at special

Gourds have been used as flasks and water canteens for literally thousands of years.

events (e.g., races, concerts) or by banks, outdoor stores, bicycling shops, and other places.

Two challenges that need to be addressed with water containers are the issues of weight and bulk. Water weighs more than eight pounds per gallon and under normal circumstances is consumed rather quickly, requiring routine refilling of the container. Therefore, it may not be practical to store a full water container *inside* the kit, if we are talking about a fairly compact kit. What you might be inclined to store in the kit instead are water-collecting devices, filtering or purifying products, materials to make a solar still, or whatever you decide will help provide fresh water during survival emergencies in your neck of the woods.

One exception to this is the disposable zip-seal plastic bag we talked about earlier—you can use it to carry water. It

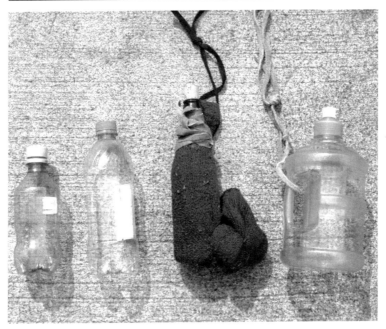

Examples of common low-cost "canteens" include the two disposable soft drink bottles at left, the beer bottle in a protective boot sock capped with a wine bottle cork, and the plastic bottle with carry handle at far right.

Here is that same Ziploc bag we saw in chapter 1 housing a survival kit, only now it is used as a water canteen!

may not be the sturdiest water bag you will ever find, but in my experiment I found it will hold water without leaking, and the bag I used resisted popping to a surprising degree. The beauty of it is that an empty plastic bag or two can conveniently be stored in most medium-sized kits, is relatively inexpensive, and is a wonderfully versatile product in the wilderness, being useful for carrying things as well as keeping important small items dry and easy to find.

WATER COLLECTION AND TREATMENT NEEDS

While we're on this subject of providing ourselves access to fresh water in an emergency, we should contemplate some methods for capturing fresh water and filtering and purifying the questionable water supplies we are most likely to encounter in the wilderness.

The first option is the simplest: set out whatever drinking containers and vessels you have in the rain to collect fresh water that won't generally require filtration or purification.

The clear plastic sheeting you might be packing in your kit for expedient tarp shelters could also be used to capture and channel rainwater into your drinking containers or build one or more solar stills like we see in almost every outdoor survival book, which could conceivably help you collect some fresh water where other sources may be questionable. If you plan to have this option available, you will want some type of drinking tube or straw through which to extract any collected water without having to tear the apparatus apart. Latex rubber surgical tubing is flexible and not extremely expensive in lengths of only several feet long (often sold in sporting goods stores with the fishing tackle), and the same product could also find use in slingshots, as we will talk more about in chapter 9.

The simple, old-fashioned—and most reliable—method for purifying bacteria-contaminated water is to boil it to kill the bacteria, and this would be my first choice whenever building a fire is possible or you have access to some other heat source.

Latex rubber surgical tubing might be suitable as a solar still drinking tube, is flexible enough to coil into a small roll, and elastic enough to be used in slingshot bands.

However, it may not always be possible, practical, or convenient to make a fire and boil water under certain emergency circumstances, but the only available water source could nevertheless be contaminated. For this type of scenario, the chemical treatment approach is a viable one. Chlorine, iodine crystals, iodine-based tablets, tincture of iodine liquid, halazone tablets, and silver ion tablets have all been used for purifying water, with varying degrees of success.

There are two good things about most of the products currently available for this purpose: 1) a tiny bottle or packet of purification pills is compact and lightweight and will fit into most survival kits, and 2) one small container of water purification tabs will not break your bank, with prices running $4 to $6 per 50-count bottle at camping supply stores, and a small bottle of iodine tincture typically even less at the local supermarket.

This tiny glass bottle from Potable Aqua contains 50 water purification tablets.

The potential downside of the chemicals is that not everyone can safely ingest them, even in the limited doses required to sanitize the water. Also, you have the issue of shelf life to consider. According to the FAQ page on the Potable Aqua website, the shelf life of their chlorine dioxide water purification tablets is four years, and they recommend checking the exact expiration date on the package. Once the bottle has been opened, the lifespan of the tablets' effectiveness will be very limited after being exposed to the air.

Pumps with ceramic filters represent another method for making suspect water safe to drink, and they have become enormously popular with recreational hikers. However, the good ones are really too large to fit into small survival kits, and they are relatively expensive.

In a wilderness environment, it is possible to fabricate a makeshift filter to process dirty water, using a sock, for example, and filling it with layers of grass, charcoal from the campfire, and sand from an uncontaminated area. Something along this order might filter out the bigger sediments and slime, but it cannot be trusted to remove or destroy dangerous bacteria.

CHAPTER FOUR

POOR MAN'S WILDERNESS COOKWARE

It could be argued that cookware is not absolutely essential to human survival, and I would not disagree. We can roast trout or squirrel on a green stick over an open campfire without having to use a frying pan, for instance. However, if you need to boil stagnant swamp water in order to make it safe to drink, or stir ingredients together to produce a special concoction of one kind or another, then a metal pot can seem like a godsend.

COOKING VESSELS

Expedient cook pots and mess kits are not difficult to create or adapt from common materials. The ubiquitous disposable metal coffee can, for example, has been adapted to serve as hobo stoves, cook pots, and water pails for decades. And as was suggested in chapter 1, a steel coffee can that has been cleaned and saved as an expedient survival cook pot could also serve as the main kit container, making a very convenient and portable compact storage canister for all of those smaller survival items.

This lightweight camp cook pot/frying pan was makeshift from a 2-lb. steel coffee can, cut to the desired height and its lip sanded smooth, with a coat hanger wire attached for a handle.

The large size (usually 2 1/4-lb.) steel coffee can serves as a wonderful little wood cook stove. I built mine by first drilling a series of holes all around the sides of the can for ventilation, and then cutting a little window near the base on one side to make it easier to feed in the small pieces of wood to fuel it. The smallest 6-inch round steel or aluminum tent stakes work as grate bars and for creating a shelf a few inches above the floor of the stove to facilitate easier burning, but any heavy metal wire or small-diameter steel rod would suffice for these grate bars, which are pushed through small holes either drilled or punched through the sides of the can where desired.

The thin steel these coffee cans are comprised of produces sharp edges wherever cut or drilled, so I spent some time folding the edges inward, hammering some of them down flat using a small ball peen hammer, and sanding some of them as smooth as I could. I also used the jaws of my Leatherman multitool to grab the tallest burrs and pull them free.

I have noticed that many of the new steel coffee cans have a lip inside the rim of the opening (1/4-inch wide inside the

Above: Two modified metal coffee cans being used to boil water. The top is an 11-oz. can with a strip of metal soldered to the side to create a mug with a handle. The 2 1/4-lb. can under it has holes cut into the sides and a coat hanger wire grate across its opening to create a charcoal heater.

Above right: This makeshift coffee can wood stove has an opening cut into its side for feeding fresh fuel and holes for ventilation, plus steel rods inserted for the grate and fuel shelf. Fire starter (e.g., paper, tinder) goes in the bottom, wood on the fuel shelf, and cooking vessel on the top grate.

Right: Firing up the stove to boil water.

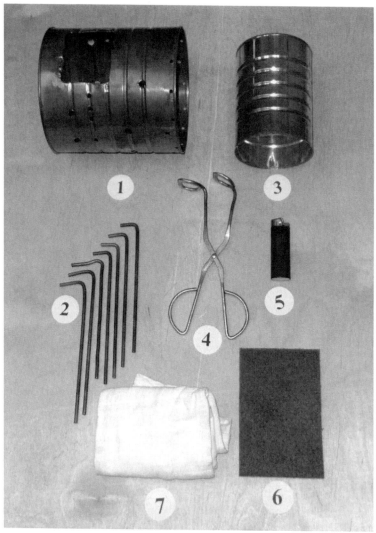

The components that comprise the coffee can wood stove cook kit: 1) Large coffee can modified to function as a wood stove, 2) grate rods made from 3/16-inch diameter steel rod, although small metal tent stakes would also work, 3) 11-oz. coffee can for boiling water and cooking, 4) hot dog tongs modified to grip edge of hot coffee can, 5) cigarette lighter, 6) abrasive scrub pad for cleaning the cook pot, and 7) cloth towel/dish rag for hot pad. All these components—except with different tongs than those shown here—stow inside the stove, and a plastic lid holds everything inside.

Stove kit packed up inside can.

11-oz. cans; 3/8 inch in the large cans). This can be an awkward feature for our purposes, making it more difficult to grip the can's rim with tongs or pour liquid out of the can. However, this annoying lip ring is easy to remove cleanly using one of those popular new types of can openers or even the jaws of a Leatherman tool. Once removed, flatten the remaining sharp edges inside the opening with a small hammer; hit all the way around the circumference while slowly rotating the can with the side of its rim against a hard surface. Smooth up a bit afterward with sandpaper.

Coat hanger wire can be useful in conjunction with steel coffee cans, serving as expedient grate bars in stoves if heavier steel bars are not available, or as a wraparound can holder when twisted up to form rigid handles. A simple bail for a coffee can is also very practical and easy to make out of a coat hanger.

The inside lip ring is easily and cleanly removed using a modern can opener.

Removing the lip from inside the rim of an 11-oz. steel coffee can using pliers. Here I am using a Leatherman, but any sturdy pair of needle-nose or ordinary pliers will do.

Above: How a simple coat hanger wire bail can be hooked into two small holes near the rim of the can.

Right: The wire bail can be bent into a smaller loop for stowing inside the can.

Below: Simple, utilitarian bowl formed in aluminum foil.

A very temporary vessel for boiling water could be improvised in a pinch from a sheet of aluminum foil, especially the heavy-duty foil, and it is lightweight enough to find a place in most wilderness kits. Alternatively, a foil baking pan could thusly be used, and one or two of these could be folded flat and stuffed into a medium-size kit. Foil pans are not expensive, incredibly lightweight, and can be found in every supermarket.

The biggest drawback to the foil pan for an emergency kit is that, once folded and unfolded, it develops weak points along the fold seams and will usually tear or break in those places if folded again, at least in my experience. So this is a one-time-use proposition, and a marginal one at that. Nevertheless, it is possible to boil water in one of these things, so it is worth considering for that purpose.

While you are scouring those yard sales for those survival kit knives and packs mentioned earlier, you might as

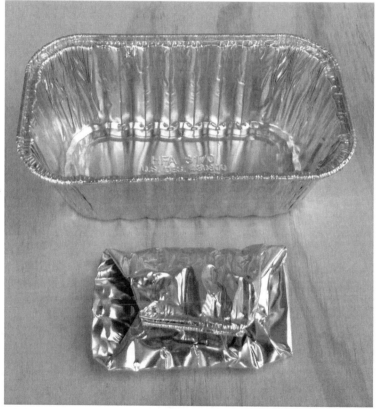

A baking foil pan can be folded into a fairly flat shape for stowing in the kit and later opened back up into a usable pan when needed for boiling water.

Miscellaneous items of cookware acquired at yard sales for pennies on the dollar. This is a super cheap way to assemble your complete camp kitchen.

well keep your eyes open for cookware. It is impossible to visit a series of yard sales without encountering kitchen stuff, and most of what I've seen has been priced very low because the people usually just want to get rid of it in favor of newer, shinier products. Good, usable gear for the wilderness never needs to be expensive—it's going to get dirty and banged up out there anyway. The key will be to find something usable for camp that will also fit into whatever size kit you plan to assemble.

METHODS FOR HANDLING HOT POTS AND PANS

Having a coffee can or other metal pot in which to boil water can make a dramatic difference in your existence in the wild, but you will also need some means by which to safely handle and manage the hot cooking vessel.

A leather glove on the hand or a folded cloth rag could

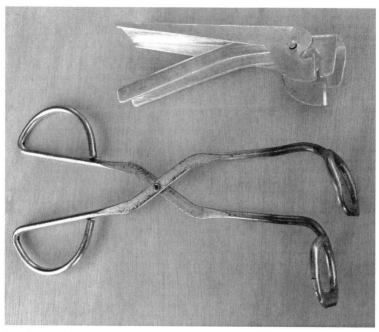

Two inexpensive gripping tools suitable for our mess kits: an aluminum pot holder (at top) and hot dog tongs with jaws bent to more easily grip the rim of a tin can.

serve as an expedient hot pad at the campfire, but some type of metal gripping tool is hard to beat for managing hot containers. A common pair of pliers might serve in a pinch, but a gripping tool with a longer handle specifically designed for this purpose is ideal.

For my coffee can camp stove, I modified a pair of 25¢ thrift store hot dog tongs by bending the jaws downward to facilitate gripping the rim of the can. It works, but not as effectively as those compact aluminum pot holder/gripper tools sold in all of the camping supply stores. The nice thing about the aluminum camping pot holder, besides being cheap, is that it has short enough handles to fit inside the small-size coffee can for storage.

The compact $2 camper pot gripper works very well and will fit inside a small coffee can for storage.

Using the modified hot dog tongs to lift a water-filled can.

ALCOHOL STOVES FOR THE SURVIVAL KIT

Compact cook stoves that burn alcohol have been a practical choice for backpackers for a long time, and homemade stoves from aluminum pop cans have become popular in recent years. These little burners are easy to make, cost nothing, weigh almost nothing, take up very little space in the kit, and make efficient use of their fuel.

You can find various designs on countless websites, but a very practical and easy-to-build soda can (or beer can) alcohol stove that I have experimented with lately, and one that is made entirely from a single aluminum can, was described by Alan Halcon in his article for the now out-of-print magazine *Wilderness Way* (volume 10, issue 3, circa 2004), titled "The Halconstove." In that article, Mr. Halcon—a regular personality today on the outdoor survival/primitive skills website Dirt Time (http://dirttime.com/)—explains how to build the stove he designed with its ingenious vapor chamber. It requires only a sharp knife for the entire task, although I found that using a pair of large scissors for some of the steps results in straighter cut edges and components that fit together better.

This fairly crude alcohol stove was fabricated using only the blade of a knife for a tool.

Mr. Halcon provided detailed, easy-to-follow instructions with his article, but for this discussion I will highlight the main steps involved in building this excellent little stove. Hopefully it will be enough, in conjunction with the accompanying photos, to help the readers figure it out.

The first step is to scratch a line with the point of a blade around the entire circumference of the can 1 inch up from the bottom of the can. Then scratch another line around the circumference 1½ inches down from the top of the can. (It is easiest to flip the can upside down for scratching this line.) Finally, scratch a third line around the top ¼ inch down from the top where the shoulder begins to slope toward the rim.

Before progressing to the next step, poke slits into the aluminum with the tip of your blade (a clip-point blade is ideal for this) along this third line, about 1/8-inch long and about 1/8-inch apart. Also, now is the best time to remove the inside lid (that contains the pull-tab) by scoring along the circular groove inside the lip with the knife and cutting and prying out that thin disk.

Now, carefully cut off the bottom 1-inch section of the can at the scratch line; then cut off the top 1 1/2-inch section so that you are now left with three separate detached sections of your original aluminum can. Cut up one side (vertically) of the center tubular section to form a rectangular strip. Trim this strip down to a height of 1 7/8 inch (an eighth under 2 inches) by cutting straight along its entire length. Its final dimensions should now be 1 7/8 inches tall by 8 1/2 inches long.

Roll this middle section into a tube of roughly 2 inches in diameter with some overlapping of its ends so that it fits into the narrow circular channel in the underside of the top section of the can. Cut a 3/16-inch square tab in the overlapped area that folds over and locks the overlapping ends of the tube together, and cut three more evenly spaced tabs in that end of the tube, which will serve as flow gates for the fuel in the finished stove.

The final step before assembly is to gently corrugate (with your fingers) the cut top edge of the bottom section such that

The three separate sections of the soda can stove: bottom, middle, and top. Note how the sides of the bottom section have been corrugated, as well as the tabs cut into the middle section.

Fitting the pieces together.

A view of the tubular middle section fitted into the narrow circular channel in the underside of the top section.

it will slide without a fight into the top section. Then all that is required is fitting the three pieces together, pouring the alcohol into the center, and lighting it with a match or lighter.

It is possible to set a small pot or vessel directly on the tiny soda can stove for cooking, but it won't be very stable. Fortunately, it is not difficult to improvise a small stand or grill for this purpose. I modified a used potato masher I found in a box of goodies at a yard sale by cutting its handle off and straightening the two remaining arms to form a little grill that can be shoved into the dirt right over the alcohol stove.

The obvious downside to any stove that burns store-bought fuel is that it requires hauling the fuel around with the stove rather than simply collecting and burning the endless dry wood at the campsite. Even so, a 12-oz. bottle of alcohol will keep one of these tiny stoves heating for quite awhile, and it will burn cleaner and more efficiently than any wood stove. Besides, the stove

Above: Potato masher from yard sale.

Right: Makeshift grill from potato masher, shoved into the dirt over stove. Just light the alcohol in the stove and set the pan on top.

The fuel for a backpacker's alcohol stove, with a makeshift—and clearly labeled—storage container.

itself is ultralightweight and more compact than any other cook stove I have ever seen.

Denatured alcohol is suitable for use in alcohol stoves, but rubbing alcohol (isopropyl alcohol) and alcoholic beverages will not burn efficiently enough for this purpose. I tried this stove with such other fuels as lamp oil and lighter fluid, and while I believe they *could* be used for the task in a pinch, they will clearly not work as effectively with this system as the denatured alcohol. (For example, in my experiment the

Burning denatured alcohol in the soda can stove.

lighter fluid seemed to burn up too quickly.) The flame of burning alcohol is sometimes hard to see outdoors, but it burns long and steadily nevertheless, and is not easily extinguished by a hard wind.

Denatured alcohol is found in the paint department of most hardware stores, as it is used as a solvent. A 32-oz. can will typically cost around $6, depending on which brand and where it is sold. Remember that fire safety will always merit your close attention whenever dealing with flammables.

CHAPTER FIVE

POOR MAN'S FIRE KIT

I think most experienced outdoorsmen agree that the ability to make fire is one of the most important wilderness survival functions. It makes boiling/purifying water or cooking meat possible. It provides potentially lifesaving warmth in cold weather, light by which to see in the dark, and a means for signaling. It facilitates the fire-hardening of tools and clay vessels, not to mention the forging of iron tools. And it boosts morale, arguably one of the most important factors in successful wilderness survival.

As I see it, there are basically four usable "poor man" methods for making fires in the wilderness.

FIRE BY FRICTION

The first (and most primitive) method we will consider is fire by friction. This would include such ancient methods as the bow drill, the hand drill, the fire plow, and the fire saw. We might even toss the fire piston into this category, even though technically it provides heat from compressed air as opposed to friction generated by wood rubbing against wood.

The biggest advantage of the friction fire method is that it does not depend upon any factory-made or difficult-to-find components or materials. Wherever vegetation grows, the materials for building the required tools of the fire kit exist. Hence, knowing how to create fire by friction conceivably allows a survivor to accomplish this task using only natural materials and without any money investment.

For those who've never made fire with a bow drill kit but wish to experiment with this method, the process is very simple. The

Having the ability and materials to start a fire is critical in the wilderness.

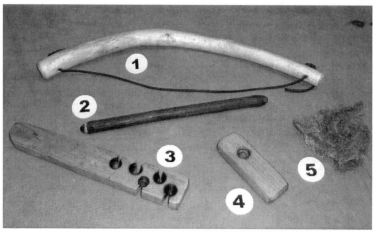

The components of the bow drill fire-making kit: 1) fire bow, 2) spindle, 3) fire board, or hearth, 4) top socket, and 5) tinder "bird's nest." This may be an awkward method for obtaining fire in the wilderness, but it could be used successfully, and its components cost no money at all.

The labor-intensive bow drill method for obtaining fire by friction is demonstrated here.

object is to get the spindle spinning rapidly and continuously, in alternating directions, in the fireboard socket with progressively increasing downward pressure. This will eventually produce a darkened charred powder and then thick, streaming smoke.

At that point, a hidden coal will exist in the powder, which will first appear as a glowing dot the size of a pinhead, but only when air is gently blown onto it. As air is steadily blown over it, the coal will grow in size. At that stage, it is just a matter of carefully transporting the charred powder with the coal to a bird's nest-like tinder bundle of dry fibers that you should be keeping ready (a small pointed twig can be very handy for picking the charred powder out of the fireboard notch), continuing to blow air onto the coal until the flames erupt within the tinder bundle. That's all there is to it.

The biggest disadvantages to this method are that it is labor intensive and very time-consuming (at least for me, because I am not as physically fit as I was 25 years ago). It takes considerable human energy to prepare and execute, and it also requires practice to master the skill.

Additionally, a bow drill fire kit is bulky for carrying compared with most other fire-making systems, because with a complete kit you've got the fire bow, the spindle shaft, the top socket, and the fireboard, as well as the supply of tinder with some means for keeping it bone dry. So this is definitely not a pocket survival kit item. Nevertheless, the tools used for creating it in an emergency—mainly a cutting tool, and cord for the bowstring—can be used for other purposes, and those compact and lightweight items *are* normally carried in every outdoor survival the kit.

THE MODERN CIGARETTE LIGHTER

While a fire bow might have been a practical component of an ancient wilderness kit, we obviously have much more efficient systems available to us now. Perhaps the easiest to use in a stressful emergency scenario, and our second fire-starting method category for this chapter, is a modern cigarette lighter. Even non-smokers know how to use cigarette lighters, and the disposable varieties are conveniently inexpensive.

Above: The famous BIC lighter comes in several sizes, is very reliable and durable for a disposable product, is found in every quick stop and grocery store, and normally costs a little more than a dollar apiece.

Left: For the serious skinflint types, the three-for-a-dollar variety will also provide a flame on demand.

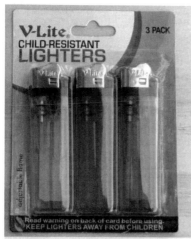

Left: Using the needle-nose jaws of the Leatherman tool to pull the childproofing metal strip off the top of the lighter.

Below: The lighter on the left has a child-proof strip, but the strip was removed from the lighter next to it. This makes it much easier for cold, numb, or gloved fingers to spin the sparking mechanism and produce a flame.

Any dollar or drug store sells them cheap by the pack; online, you can get a pack of 50 for $12, or 24 cents a lighter.

One of the first things I usually do after acquiring a disposable butane lighter is remove that thin strip of metal over the roller they all come with now that is supposed to make it childproof or child resistant. I use the needle-nose jaws of my Leatherman to grip it and pull it straight up and off the top of the lighter. This makes the product much easier for me to use in the woods with cold, numb fingers, although I cannot recommend others do this for the obvious safety reasons. My lighters are for my survival pack and not normally within easy reach of small children.

I have lost lighters in the dark around the camp, so another handy modification is to attach small lanyard cord to the body with a short strip of duct tape. Wrapping a few winds of duct tape onto the lighter also makes it easier to grip, plus it provides an additional supply of tape in your kit.

One possible hazard with the disposable lighter is that its

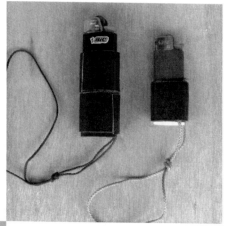

Right: Disposable lighters with cords attached to make them easier to secure, and wrapped with duct tape for an easier grip.

Below: The Zippo cigarette lighter with its lid open, ready for use.

button could inadvertently be depressed by other gear wedged against it within a tightly packed kit, causing its fuel to leak out while stowed. Then when you need its flame to save your life from hypothermia in an emergency, you discover in horror that it won't work. For this reason, it is crucial to pack the lighter in your kit with special care.

A classic, long-lasting type of cigarette lighter is the famous Zippo that uses replaceable wicks and flints and must be periodically refilled with lighter fluid to keep it operational. I love these old-school lighters with their sturdy metal cases and spring-retained lid caps, although I cannot ignore their disadvantages for our purpose. Single units cost around $10 or more nowadays, so they aren't exactly "poor man cheap." And the lighter fluid either evaporates or gets used up fairly quickly, requiring routine refills. If you are going to keep such a device in your pack, you'll need to keep a bottle of lighter fluid to store with it, and that will cost you roughly another $3, and it won't last forever.

But the neat thing about the Zippo, besides the hinged

Left: An old Zippo lighter that has been wrapped with electrical tape and two different sizes of small-diameter braided cord to provide a better grip and a cord supply.

Below: Using the Zippo as a candle. Once the flame is lit, no hands required.

cap that protects the ignition system, is that once the flame ignites, you don't have to hold any buttons down with your thumb to sustain the flame the way you do with a disposable lighter. The Zippo can stand upright on a table with its flame burning and work hands-free like a candle until the fuel is consumed.

The major drawbacks to any type of cigarette lighter are that they will no longer provide a flame when their fuel is consumed, and at least with most products on the market, they don't work very well or at all when completely wet. It is often suggested that the sparking mechanism may still provide a means for igniting tinder after the lighter's fuel has been consumed, but I have not had any success with this technique, so I consider it an iffy proposition under adverse conditions.

As an experiment to simulate a hard rain, I have run cold water from the kitchen faucet across the top of a disposable lighter for at least a full minute to find out how this affects its performance. In every one of my trials, the lighter has refused to spark at all until the water in the mechanism completely dried. The good news is that this usually only took about five minutes when periodically blowing air over the top of the lighter, and after it dries out, the unit normally is completely operational again.

THE SULFUR MATCH

Matches constitute my least favorite method for obtaining fire under desperate circumstances, mainly because I don't always trust my ability to reliably start a fire with them when the conditions aren't ideal. Nevertheless, they are a popular ignition system that everyone knows how to use, and in limited quantities they are truly inexpensive, so we have to explore their possibilities here. Let's take a look at several variations of the traditional sulfur match.

Wooden kitchen matches can be effectively waterproofed to make them more usable in the wilderness in any of several ways, from painting the heads with nail polish to dipping them in hot wax. The only company I am aware of that produces the strike-anywhere type these days is Diamond, distributed by Jarden Home Brands. This product may be restricted and difficult to find in some jurisdictions, or so I've heard, but I still find them sold in several stores in my area. The strike-anywhere kitchen matches we used to buy years

Three varieties of matches, from left: Diamond "Strike Anywhere" wooden kitchen matches that will ignite when their tips are scraped across most types of abrasive surfaces; the typical book-type matches that normally require striking against the strip on the book; and specially coated weather-resistant "Stormproof" stick matches intended for outdoor survival—which cost considerably more than the other types.

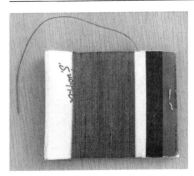

Book of matches wrapped with sewing thread to make it more worthy of its space in the kit.

ago were the Ohio Blue Tips, and I liked them better because they had noticeably larger tips.

Book matches are smaller, will not usually sustain a flame as long as a wooden stick match, and require that strip on the book for striking, but they are also very cheap. Consisting mostly of cardboard and paper, they will not survive very well in wet conditions. If you keep a few books of matches in your kit, it will be wise to store them in a small plastic zip-seal bag to keep them dry. You may also want to wind some thread around a book of matches to make the item more worthy of its space in your kit.

SPARKING FIRE IGNITERS

Spark-producing fire igniters fall into two categories: the contemporary ferrocerium sparkers that can be scraped using any edge of steel to produce super hot sparks, and the quartzite rock (usually flint) used in conjunction with carbon steel to produce sparks. This second category was the standard method used for firearms ignition (with flintlocks) for over 200 years.

My two favorite things about any sparking system for igniting fires are: 1) it will last for hundreds and probably even thousands of strikes before the product is worn out, and 2) it will throw sparks in all weather extremes in my experience, to some degree even if it gets damp. The tinder does have to be suitable to hold a spark, and this is perhaps the biggest concern with any sparking system.

Modern sparking devices that use ferrocerium are desirable because they throw incredibly hot sparks, and they can

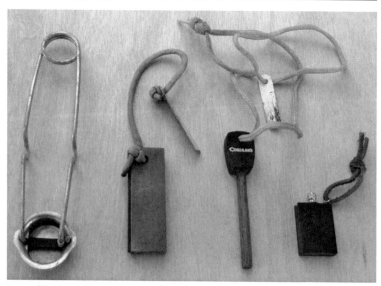

Several igniters that use ferrocerium, from left: traditional welding torch igniter with its typical hardware store price in 2012 of about $2.50 for the basic model; magnesium block with hacksaw blade scraper that will cost about $7 in most outdoor supply stores, and the magnesium can be scraped off into a pile of shavings in damp weather to serve as super-hot tinder fuel; Coughlan's ferrocerium rod fire starter that was purchased for $4.50; and the Chinese-made "Flint Match" with its embedded ferrocerium bar in one edge and steel striker rod that screws into the top. These are very compact and, for less than $4 apiece, also come with a supply of paraffin-saturated tinder balls.

Close-up of these tiny imported flint matches. The diagram on the box shows how they work.

be scraped with the sharp edge of different types of hard materials (not necessarily steel). A ball of plant-fiber tinder resembling a bird's nest, lint from the clothes dryer, cotton balls, or even fine steel wool can be ignited by the hot sparks these devices generate.

I discovered that ferrocerium is fairly brittle and can easily break if dropped. I dropped one of the Coghlan's 5/16-inch-diameter rods on a gravel driveway and a 2-inch section of the end broke off. If this ever happens to you, don't sweat it. Simply turn that broken product into two usable units. I used JB Weld to glue that 2-inch section into a hole I drilled in the tip of a cow horn for a handle and added a length of parachute cord as a lanyard. Even the short (7/8-inch long) section remaining with the original handle sparks like the Fourth of July when scraped.

The traditional flint and steel fire kit consisted of a piece of actual flint rock having a sharp edge for scraping and a piece of high-carbon steel properly tempered. For the tinder, a supply of charred cotton cloth normally was used because it will catch and sustain a tiny spark more effectively than will a

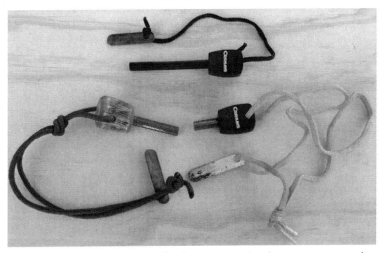

A broken ferrocerium rod—just like the top example when new—was used to make the two shorter fire tools at bottom. The one at left has the cow horn handle. All three work perfectly.

Flint and steel fire kit, including (left to right) flint rock, steel, and charred cloth tinder—three variations of steel are shown here.

Using the flint and steel to throw sparks onto the charred cloth.

bundle of dry plant fibers. The sparks generated by the striking of flint against steel will not be as hot or as bright as those generated by scraping ferrocerium.

Even so, this is a viable method for this discussion because you could devise your own kit without having to buy anything factory-made, assuming you can find a source of high-carbon steel suitable for sparking and a quartzite rock like flint or chert. And you will have to char some patches of cloth for the tinder. For the steel component of the kit, I nor-

This flint and steel kit consists of the bag to house all of it, the steel made from a round file, the piece of flint, leather pad to protect the fingers from the sharp rock, and the charred cloth patches stored in a homemade leather wallet.

The flint and steel kit packed up inside its own little bag, ready for adventure!

mally use old, worn-out round files and grind the teeth off the scrape side, sometimes heating them in my forge and shaping as desired before retempering.

TINDER

We all know that having some sort of flame- or spark-producing tool with us in the wilderness will be crucial, but I think almost equally important—though not as routinely thought of as the main fire tool—is the dry tinder. If you lack the right fuel for your fire when the time comes—such as in wet or very cold conditions—you will surely struggle in desperation and your situation could become very dire in a hurry. A supply of tinder in a waterproof container belongs in every serious outdoor survival kit, in my opinion.

It was mentioned above that sparks produced by flint rock striking against carbon steel require special tinder for ignition, ideally charred cotton cloth to catch and sustain the sparks. Cloth patches are easy

Above: Charred cloth patches in the small metal can in which they were charred.

Left: A spark has ignited this piece of charred cloth. Blow on it to sustain the heat and light your tinder.

Cotton balls and petroleum jelly for do-it-yourself tinder balls on the left, store-bought tinder balls on the right.

to char by enclosing them in an oxygen-starved environment such as a small metal canister with only a small pinhole in the cap to allow the expanding gases to escape. Heat the container over the campfire or on the kitchen stove until an actual flame replaces the smoke that escapes from the pinhole during the process. When the flame appears, the cloth is charring, and it is then time to move the canister away from the heat source and allow it to cool. In my experience, the darker the char, the better it will catch the sparks.

Hotter sparks, such as those produced by scraping ferrocerium, will readily ignite a variety of tinder materials. The fluff from cattails, dry mosses, and fuzzy tree bark are just a few examples of excellent natural tinder materials found in the wild. You could buy fuel-impregnated tinder balls at any sporting goods store, but you can also prepare your own by saturating inexpensive cotton balls with petroleum jelly, which you can keep dry in a zip-lock plastic bag. When it comes time to use them for starting your fire, simply pull the fibers apart just enough to allow plenty of air circulation between them and shower the ball with sparks. Fine steel wool is another popular fire-starting tinder that can be ignited with sparks from ferrocerium.

CHAPTER SIX

POOR MAN'S SHELTER

Shelter is a basic human necessity, and protecting ourselves from the elements can be lifesaving. Complete shelter systems are usually not included in the smallest survival kits, being way too bulky, but some of the tools and materials for making them (e.g., cutting tools, cord, plastic sheeting) typically will be.

We've already talked about cutting tools, and when it comes to shelter building, these invariably will be useful for such tasks as cutting and notching lean-to frame pieces and so forth. Even if you don't have to use a cutting tool to harvest tree branches for your shelter, you will probably need to cut lengths of cord for lashings, guy lines, or simple tie-downs, depending upon the type of shelter you build. A cutting tool in your kit makes these tasks quick and easy.

PLASTIC BAGS AND SHEETS

Something as seemingly irrelevant as a plastic trash bag can make a huge difference in your outdoor experience. Large plastic bags, especially those heavy-duty 33-gallon and larger bags used a

Left: A small, low-to-the-ground tent-type shelter improvised from a single large, opened-up plastic trash bag and lengths of cord. It does shed water and provide shade under the sun, but it makes for a fairly delicate shelter.

Below: A plastic trash bag serving here as an expedient rain jacket or wind breaker.

lot for landscaping chores and by contractors, are potentially useful as emergency windbreaks or rain-shedding devices. They are the popular poor man's poncho and tarp system, and a very expedient and temporary shelter device *could* be fabricated using them, I learned. As I described in my book *More Makeshift Workshop Skills*, I once draped several plastic trash bags over an old tent roof that was leaking during a rainy camping/fishing trip in the mountains, and those bags were successful in completely stopping the leak.

There is a considerable difference between available products. The 1 mil or less, garden-variety trash bag is certainly lightweight, inexpensive, and conveniently compact for storing in a survival kit, but it has severe limitations in my observation. It tears too easily, and it isn't large enough when opened (typically 4 feet by 5½ feet) to create a decent tarp-type shelter by itself, unless you were to duct-tape two opened bags together along one seam to double the roof area.

Also, I wouldn't expect a shelter made from such a thin

This 4- by 6-foot sheet of heavy clear plastic is folded into a compact package that will fit into a medium-sized kit, and it could serve as a poor man's tarp, solar still, or windbreak in a pinch.

bag to hold up long under very much wind. I wouldn't say they are totally worthless in a pinch, and tossing a few in your kit might give some degree of protection given their limitations. Even the lightest, easiest-to-tear trash bags can keep rain off of you. But some of the super heavy-duty, industrial-grade bags on the market—like the Husky brand "Contractor Clean-Up" bags, which are 42 gallons in size and advertised as 3-mil thick, or any of the 33- to 60-gallon 2-mil bags from International Plastics—would be well worth their volume in any medium-size wilderness survival kit. The tougher bags are more expensive, heavier in weight, and slightly bulkier than the garden variety, and they typically cost more than 50 cents per bag, but one or two of them could be a godsend in an outdoor emergency situation.

A large enough square or rectangular sheet of something like thick polyethylene plastic, PVC, Mylar, or Visqueen is another option for a lightweight and versatile tarp shelter system suitable for our poor man's survival kit. The sheet could also be used to collect rainwater anywhere; if it is clear and you are in the desert, it could potentially serve as an expedient solar still for collecting water.

CHEAP RAIN PONCHOS

Inexpensive, disposable, emergency hooded rain ponchos are sold in numerous stores I shop in, usually near the cash register with other cheap trinkets, and I had the opportunity to employ one of these products during an unexpectedly heavy, driving rainstorm while on a recent campout. Despite their marginal quality and low price, I learned firsthand that these lightweight ponchos will indeed keep at least most of the rain off and will help shield the upper body from a chilly wind. Someone happened to have purchased one of these dollar ponchos right before the trip—I'm ashamed to admit that I wasn't the one with the wisdom, in this case—and graciously

The handy-dandy 99¢ rain ponchos sold in almost every store. Compact, lightweight, very usable, and super cheap!

shared it with the rest of us as the storm developed. Several of us donned that same garment in rotation whenever we needed to venture out from under the porch of our tent during the downpour, as sadly none of us came better prepared for a rainstorm, and we were all in agreement that the cheapo import made a huge difference.

CORDAGE FOR CONSTRUCTING SHELTER

Cordage (and we'll talk more about cord in the next chapter) is every bit as useful for shelter construction as is any tarp or bag. For tent pitching and shelter building, I would recommend that every woodsmen know how to form at least two pertinent knots: 1) the hangman's knot, which creates a remarkably practical constricting noose, and 2) the taut line hitch, which allows tension adjustment to a guy line.

The only practical way I know of to attach lines to the

Rope securely attached to a corner of a plastic sheet using the constricting hangman's knot and a pebble. Easy connection to make, easy to undo, holds firmly, and will prevent cutting or tearing the sheet.

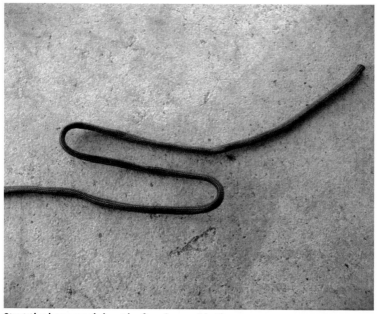

Start the hangman's knot by forming an S in the rope.

Wind the running end back over the middle of the S four or five times.

Feed the running end through the resulting eye.

Open the noose as needed and tidy up the knot. Push the knot toward the noose to constrict.

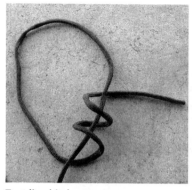

Taut line hitch, step 1.

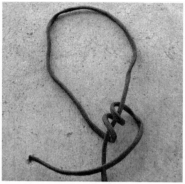

Step 2.

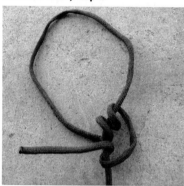

Step 3.

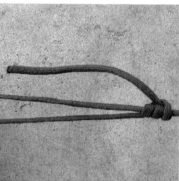

Step 4.

edges or corners of a plastic bag or sheet is to fold the section or corner of the sheet over a small, round object like a smooth pebble and then tighten the constrictor noose up around the material right behind the bulge made by the pebble so that the noose won't be able to slip off the plastic. I described the hangman's knot in *Makeshift Workshop Skills for Survival and Self-Reliance* and again in *More Makeshift Workshop Skills*, but given this knot's usefulness with improvised shelters, I cover it again here for the sake of those readers who haven't seen those books (see photos).

I learned the taut line hitch for the first time a little over a year ago while thumbing through a copy of the venerable *Boy Scout Handbook*, and I have to say that I could have used it many, many times over the years if I had only known it. If you like to go hiking and camping in the woods and have the need to set up tents and shelters, I recommend that you do yourself a huge favor and learn the taut line hitch right now and practice it often so you never forget it. Once you start using it, you'll wonder how you ever got along without it. Just follow the photo sequence.

LAST-DITCH SHELTER

If you lack a tarp, tent, plastic bag, or sheet of any kind, you should know workable methods for constructing simple lean-to shelters with or without cord, to include thatching by weaving pine boughs or other tree branches over-under/under-over to provide a tight, interlocking grid of overlapping vegetation that will hold together and shed rain or snow. First, construct a rigid framework for the shelter; then start the thatching by weaving rows of branches at the base of the wall or roof and progress upward so that the higher rows of thatch overlap the ones directly below them to allow the moisture to more effectively roll off.

This little model of a lean-to shelter illustrates the basic concept of thatched pine boughs.

CHAPTER SEVEN

SURVIVAL CORD FOR THE POOR MAN'S KIT

Cord of various sizes and materials is used routinely in more outdoor applications than I can hope to list in this book. Every outdoorsman should be a master of cordage—he should know how to fabricate usable cordage in the wild and how to use all types of cordage effectively in every conceivable application.

Although a vast assortment of cord types, from the finest threads to the heaviest ropes, are available in our modern world, we will supply ourselves with the cord we will need with only a marginal investment.

PARACHUTE CORD

Some sizes and varieties of cord are more versatile than others, and parachute cord is at the top of the heap. Most outdoorsmen are familiar with parachute cord, also called #550 cord or "paracord," with its separate (usually seven) individual nylon cords running through its core. It is talked about in almost every contemporary survival book or on-line survival blog, and rightfully so. It is the ideal small rope for tent lines, clotheslines,

A cut end of parachute cord, showing the smaller individual cords inside.

bootlaces, large animal snares, pole lashings, lanyards, trip-line perimeter alarm systems, small boat or raft anchor ropes, gear tie-down cord, expedient bowstrings, and dozens of other uses.

In 100-foot or longer lengths, the genuine military-grade parachute cord can be relatively expensive when compared with other common types of synthetic cord of similar diameter. But if you remove some of the smaller inner cords and supply several survival kits with them, you can spread the cost over more than one kit. If you can afford some genuine parachute for your survival kits, I believe the investment will be well made.

DENTAL FLOSS

Dental floss is another incredibly versatile type of thread-sized cord, being suitable as improvised fishing line, thread

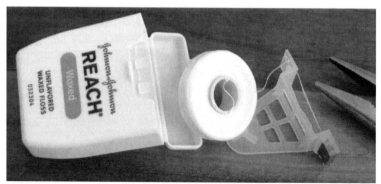

Removing the spool of floss from its bulky plastic box using needle-nose pliers.

for tying artificial flies or other fishing lures, sewing thread, small snare cord, tying arrow points to shafts, and so on. The wonderful thing about dental floss is that it is available in every grocery store, and it is relatively cheap.

I always pull the spool of floss free from the plastic box it comes in to save space in my small survival kits because the box is not needed for the kit. Instead, wrap the little spool in a small piece of aluminum foil to hold it together. Floss comes either waxed or unwaxed; I prefer the waxed version mainly because it sticks to itself and stays on the spool better, and it will hold knots much better than any unwaxed nylon thread.

SALVAGED CORDAGE

A useful collection of cords of varying materials, diameters, and lengths can be accumulated over a surprisingly short period of time by anyone endeavoring to assemble a

Scraps of miscellaneous string, thread, lace, and small rope saved from being discarded.

utilitarian wilderness kit on the cheap. If you keep your eyes open, you'll find abandoned pieces of string and rope in gardens, around dumpsters, along fences, near curbs, in parking lots, in the middle of the road, in abandoned fields, in schoolyards, at the fair, at the lake, and just about everywhere you go. In my experience, even old, weathered bootlaces and ropes will still provide usable service. Make a habit of saving what you find for your poor man's survival kit.

WIRE

Flexible wire of all sizes and configurations is salvageable from junked electrical appliances, computers, landline telephones, extension cords, electric motors, music speakers, various plastic-coated cables, and electronics of all kinds. Even nonelectrical pliable metal wire (e.g., picture-hanging wire) could be very useful for lashing shelter poles together, building snares and trip wire alarms, serving as equipment tie-

Miscellaneous electrical and nonelectrical metal wire, mostly from junked appliances. This represents a viable possibility for survival wire, and all for free.

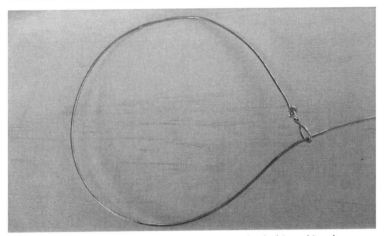

This is how simple a small animal snare noose can be fashioned in a hurry from copper wire.

down cords, or binding handles to tools. I think this is worth considering when assembling a survival kit on the cheap.

Wire coat hangers are ridiculously common and cheap, and a length of their wire loosely coiled into a circle for stowing in your survival kit could prove enormously utilitarian. We saw in chapter 4 how it can be fabricated into poor man's cookware, but it has dozens of other uses where thicker wire is beneficial, such as shelter construction. The wire is not difficult to cut using the wire cutter in my Leatherman tool or simply by bending it back and forth until it breaks.

CABLE TIES

Cable ties (also called zip ties) are commonly used for electric wiring work, but they make for fine general-purpose connectors for a survival kit. They come in various lengths, and you could fit quite a few in a medium- to large-size kit. For smaller kits, a handful could be folded into the container of choice. A pack of 100 goes for as little as $4. Cable ties have dozens of handy uses in the field, from serving as survival shelter frame connectors to making quickie repairs to broken backpack straps.

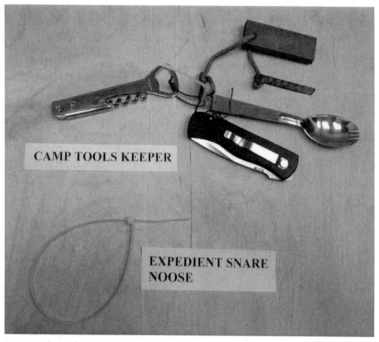

CAMP TOOLS KEEPER

EXPEDIENT SNARE NOOSE

Inexpensive cable ties are quick to connect and create a tough lock when cinched. Excellent expedient cordage for the survival kit.

MAKE YOUR OWN CORD

As we discussed at length in both *Long-Term Survival in the Coming Dark Age* and *Makeshift Workshop Skills for Survival and Self-Reliance*, simple two-ply cord is not difficult to fabricate by hand once you become comfortable with the twisting technique. There are variations to the basic method, but the main feature of all homemade cord is that multiple strands (of natural fibers, for example) are twisted together in such a way that they resist pulling apart or unraveling. In simple terms, I do this by twisting a pair of strands together in one direction while rolling each of them individually in the opposite direction so that the reverse twists in the final cord resist unraveling.

A usable small-diameter cord can be easily created from just about any flexible natural fiber by twisting individual strands together.

Hand twisting a usable supply of cord can be a tedious chore, and it is definitely time consuming. The final product has obvious limitations, having less tensile strength and durability than a lot of manufactured synthetic cords and ropes, and it will usually not be nearly as even. Nevertheless, it is another option for acquiring a supply of cord, and without any cost to you.

Hand-twisted, two-ply cord can be made using just about any pliable material or fiber. I have made usable cord out of iris leaves, knapweeds, lilac bark, tall grass of unknown variety, paper towels, duct tape, and even strips cut from plastic trash bags!

Another way for thrifty survivors to obtain usable cords, laces, straps, and the like is by cutting a spiraling ribbon from

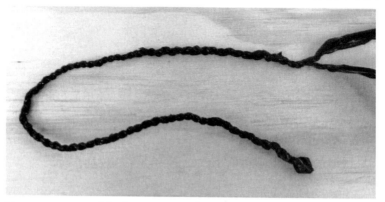

Here we see a surprisingly strong two-ply cord hand-twisted from ½-inch-wide strips cut from a black plastic trash bag. Partially stretching the narrow strips of plastic before twisting them into cord will result in a denser and firmer finished cord that will stretch less during use.

a circle of leather, rawhide, vinyl, or heavy plastic sheet with scissors or a very sharp knife. Unravel the spiral and you have a length of usable material for your binding needs.

STORING YOUR CORD

There are several practical methods for storing miscellaneous cord in your survival kits. You can wrap your tool handles, lace your boots, weave cords in and out of your pack straps or rifle slings, and use all sorts of other creative methods for ensuring you have a supply of utility cord with you at all times. For the small kits, I found that wrapping small-diameter cords and threads on flat, rigid strips of wood, plastic, or stiff cardboard makes the cord conveniently available for use while taking up a minimal amount of space inside the kits.

From my own outdoor experiences, I am convinced that a person can never really have too much cord. I find myself almost always needing more than I have with me for seemingly endless tasks in the field. An assortment of various cord sizes is a high priority in all my survival kits, and it should be in yours, too.

Miscellaneous cord and thread wrapped on various flat spools for stowing in compact kits.

CHAPTER EIGHT

POOR MAN'S IMPROVISED FISHING TACKLE

Catching fish is a viable method for acquiring food in the wild, depending on the presence of nearby lakes, ponds, streams, rivers, swamps, or coastal access. Fortunately for anyone assembling an outdoor kit, the most essential pieces of fishing tackle—the hooks, sinkers, line, and small lures—are very lightweight, at least in the limited quantities appropriate for these types of kits, and is not prohibitively expensive for the most part.

MAKESHIFT TACKLE

Even so, you can makeshift a lot of usable tackle spending hardly any money at all. Hooks, for example, can be fashioned from steel wire, safety pins, or small nails in seconds, or carved out of bone or even hardwood for those with more time on their hands. Fish could even be caught, as they have for eons, using a simple and easy-to-make toggle or gorge hook (also referred to as a "skewer hook" in FM 21-76, *U.S. Army Survival Manual*), which consists merely of a line attached to the middle of a short section of wire or stick pointed on each end. This was a common configuration for a fishhook in primitive times.

Packages of fishhooks with leader line attached are very often dirt cheap. These cost 19 cents.

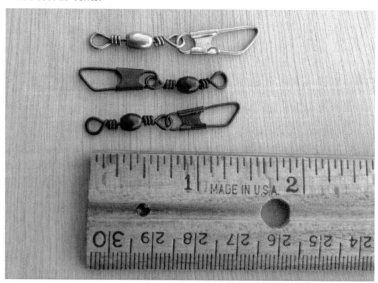

Swivels are tiny, cheap, and weigh next to nothing. They are easy to attach and are enormously beneficial for preventing tangled line. They belong in all outdoor survival kits that include fishing gear.

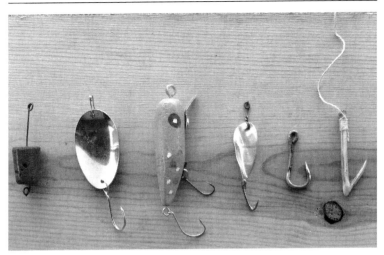

A few possibilities for homemade fishing tackle, from left: a cork and paper-clip bobber, a spoon lure shaped from a tablespoon, hand-carved wooden bass plug sporting factory-made hooks, a pull-tab spiraling spoon, coat hanger wire fishhook, and a wooden hook.

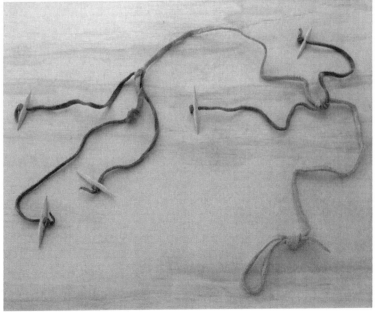

Homemade fish stringer made from wooden toggle-type gill hooks and leather cord.

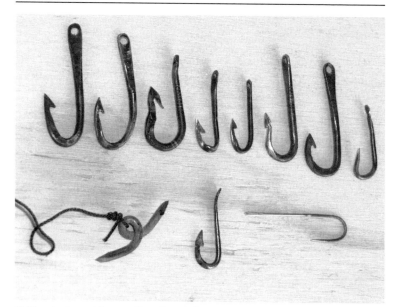

Fishhooks forged from nails, wire, and a sewing needle. The one at bottom left is an example of a toggle hook improvised from an ordinary nail.

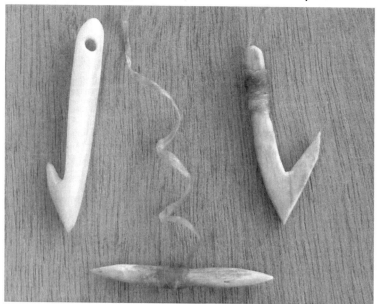

Fishhooks shaped out of bone.

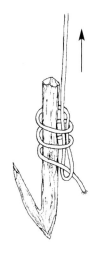

Flies and lures are fun to make out of things like feathers, thread, strips of shiny metal, wooden dowels, and various other odds and ends. You can basically invent your own lures that resemble insects, minnows, worms, or tiny frogs and, under the right conditions, expect them to actually work. A lot of effective fishing tackle is easy to improvise if you use your creativity, and the important thing is that you can assemble these items with little or no money investment.

How to tie line to a homemade fishhook. Winding the line around the hook's shank a few more times than depicted in the illustration will provide a more secure connection.

Expect some of these makeshift fish tackle items to perform better than others, and a degree of experimentation will help determine what works best in local waters. I have caught trout on my own homemade hooks and lures, so I have some confidence knowing it can be done.

HOMEMADE FISH SPEAR

You might find a fish spear useful in a survival situation. As long as you have some kind of tool with which to cut and shape available wood, along with some lengths of small-diameter cord, strong thread, or wire, you can create a fish spear fairly easily in the wilderness. Just remember to fashion barbs on the prongs in order to hold the fish on the spear so that you don't lose your dinner!

An easy way to devise a smaller fish spear or frog gig is to unbend two large barbed fishhooks to form the prongs and then secure these to a long stick with cord. I discovered that the big hooks are much easier to straighten with pliers after heating them with a propane torch as opposed to bending them cold. I inserted a nail into the end of the stick, cut off

An example of an expedient wooden fish spear that could be fabricated in the wilderness. The middle prong spears the fish and the two outer prongs secure it so it can't slip off the spear.

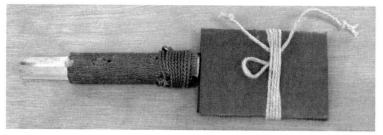

Points of frog gig protected with cardboard cover.

the head, and then sharpened the end, which helps hold the fish or frog on the spear.

The makeshift spearhead could be designed such that it is removable from the long stick. This makes it easier to pack independently in the kit and fit it to any long stick found and adapted in the field. It can be held in position with wraps of cord or even cross-pinned with a couple of small nails if any are available.

This makeshift spear should be considered as an emergency tool only, subject to any local restrictions concerning fish spearing or using barbed gigs.

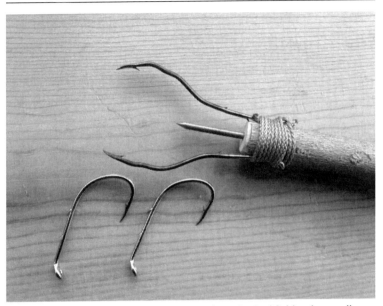

Small fish spear or frog gig made from two large barbed fishhooks, small cord, a stick, and a nail.

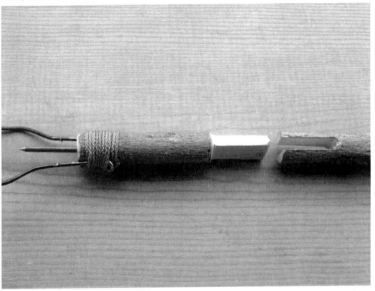

The fish spear's head piece is designed to be removable from the long stick, as seen here.

POOR MAN'S
SURVIVAL
WEAPONS

I f suddenly thrown into a survival situation in almost any remote location, one of my first priorities would be to devise some type of weapon. I know that my ability to defend myself against wild animals or predatory humans could be a determining factor in my survival, so I take this matter seriously. I am also mindful that my ability to acquire meat for food will depend to a large degree on the effectiveness of my hunting tools or weapons.

Homemade or expedient weapons normally are easily obtainable for even a poor man. In a remote wilderness environment, a survivor might be forced to devise usable weaponry from natural materials. Things like clubs, spears, slings, slingshots, blowguns, atlatls, or bows and arrows might have to serve the purpose.

I always prefer carrying firearms as opposed to going unarmed while tromping about in the woods, but a guy existing on a shoestring may not be able to afford an expensive firearm, and additionally, not all survival kits are configured to accommodate something as large as even a small handgun. For whatever reason, you may not have access to your favorite survival firearms during a wilderness

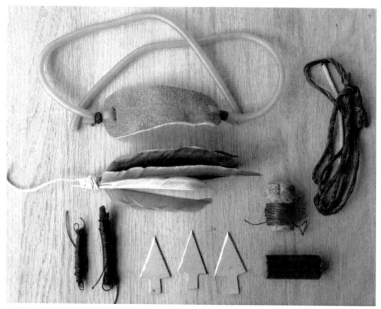

Makeshift weapon components for the survival kit: slingshot rubber with pouch, bird feathers ready for arrow fletching, a bowstring, B50 waxed cord (wrapped around a cork in this case) for making bowstrings or tying feathers or arrowheads to shafts, strong thread, duct tape for expedient arrow fins, and sheet metal arrow points.

emergency, so you should consider some alternatives appropriate for your kit or that you could assemble in an emergency with the help of tools and materials kept in your kit.

BOW AND ARROWS

Something the size of a bow with several arrows will not fit into most wilderness survival kits, but the *components* of that type of weapon system will fit into any but the tiniest of kits, and this is logical forward planning, in my view. You could prepare some of those hard-to-find (or slow-to-construct) components now and store them in your kit, making the weapon assembly much quicker and easier during a survival situation.

Makeshift broadheads cut from sheet metal would be very effective on the ends of your arrow shafts that you could fabricate in the field. These may not be legal for hunting in your region, but your survival kit is for survival emergencies.

In most of my small survival kits, I keep bowstrings, or at least a supply of waxed Dacron thread for making bowstrings in an emergency. If you don't want to pay for commercial arrowheads, you can fashion your own by cutting them out of sheet metal with a hacksaw and then grinding or filing the edges sharp. These can be fastened to scavenged or improvised arrow shafts in a survival situation, ideally tied on with

Above left: Fitting the sheet metal point into a slot cut in the end of the arrow shaft.

Above: Wrapping thread around the shaft and tang of the arrowhead.

Left: Task of affixing arrowhead completed.

strong thread. Some precut bird feathers for expedient arrow fletching will merit a place in the kit, being lightweight and compact, since it could take a while to find enough bird feathers in the wild for the task.

The fletching of arrow shafts can be accomplished in any of several makeshift ways, from tying bird feathers to the shaft as suggested above, to adhering three strips of duct tape lengthwise to the shaft and to each other evenly and then trimming with scissors to form the fins. Having these few, inexpensive materials in your survival kit can make a huge difference when the time comes to assemble your expedient archery tackle in the field.

Bird feathers were split in half and then tied to the rear part of this shaft.

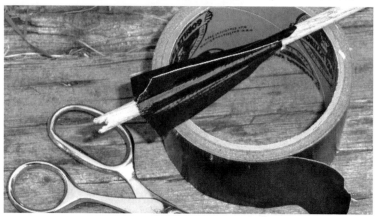

Three fins formed from duct tape for the arrow fletching.

SLINGSHOT

The materials for fabricating various other simple weapon systems in the field could also be stowed conveniently in the kit. One such practical item would be a band

Three expedient slingshots made from Y-shaped tree branches. The nice thing about slingshots is that their convenient ammo—marble-sized stones— is free and in endless supply almost everywhere.

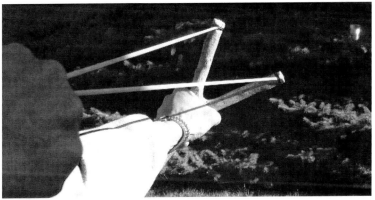

Taking aim with a homemade slingshot. That tin can on the tree branch is dead meat!

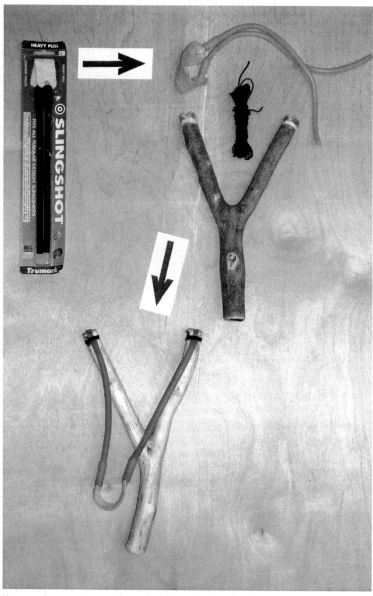

Keep an inexpensive replacement slingshot band and some strong cord in your kit for fabricating an operational weapon in the wilderness in a hurry.

Homemade slingshot utilizing flat rubber bands rather than latex tubing.

comprised of two lengths of latex surgical rubber tubing attached at the ends of a leather strap/pouch and ready for quickie slingshot fabrication in the wild.

Surgical tubing band is perfectly suited for tying to a Y-shaped branch, and it can usually be found in most sporting goods stores as slingshot replacement bands for around $3 or less. This improvised slingshot can be effective for harvesting birds, squirrels, rabbits, or other small animals at close range.

Alternatively, large, flat rubber bands could be included in the kit for the same purpose as the surgical tubing, as long as they have the sufficient elasticity. The old automobile inner tube rubber that kids often used in their slingshots in generations past would fit the bill.

SLING

A throwing sling can be a very effective and deadly primitive weapon for someone who has mastered the skill to use it. This is the weapon that David used to kill the giant Goliath in

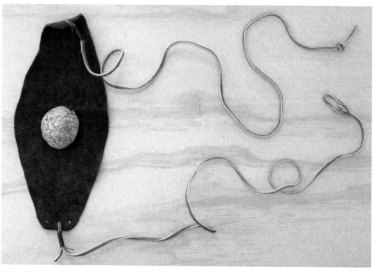

This shows how simple a throwing sling weapon is: just a leather pouch, two cords, and a rock.

the Bible. The same concept was used in conjunction with the throwing arms of medieval trebuchet-type catapults to hurl huge boulders at castles.

A sling is one of the simplest weapon systems I can think of. It is comprised of a pouch with cords attached at each end with which to swing and fling the stone projectile. One of the cords typically has a loop or ring at the end to keep it securely on the finger or fingers of the throwing hand, and the other cord will have a knotted position to facilitate gripping it between the fingers of the throwing hand until the point of release that sends the stone hurling toward the target. Round or oval stones roughly the size of chicken eggs serve well as projectiles, and they normally have enough mass to cause considerable damage to whatever objects (or creatures) they impact.

You will need some open space to practice with this weapon. When I was a kid, I learned that its effective range could easily be well over a hundred yards. It is important to

111 • POOR MAN'S SURVIVAL WEAPONS • 111

One way to attach the cords to the sling pouch is by feeding them through two holes in each end of the pouch—as opposed to one hole—and joining the cord to itself with a hangman's knot, as shown here.

stay a safe distance from bystanders, houses, schools, cars, pets, or other things you prefer not demolishing, because the stones tend to fly with great force in unpredictable directions during the learning curve. It is also possible to inadvertently wallop yourself with the stone if the release is not executed correctly.

Experiment with cord and pouch materials, pouch dimensions, cord length, and attachment methods. Pliable leather is popularly used for sling pouches, but heavy canvas, denim, or other tough materials could also serve. Any strap, bootlace, or small-diameter rope with sufficient tensile strength like parachute cord could serve as the cords. The shorter the cord length, the easier it will be to sling small projectiles accurately at close range, but longer cords will facilitate more range with heavier stones. I've come to prefer cords no longer than 16 to 18 inches for my slinging technique.

I don't remember where or when I first heard about the possibility of using an army field-dressing bandage as a

Army field-dressing bandage as issued in sealed plastic wrapper.

The bandage stretched out.

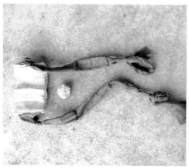

Above: The bandage prepared as a throwing sling, with a rock for its projectile.

Right: Preparing to launch the stone with the field-dressing bandage.

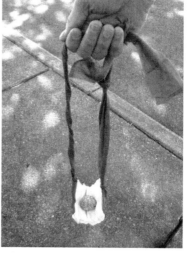

throwing sling, but as a quickie expedient I can see how it could be made to work. The bandage pad forms the pouch, and the tie strings serve as the cords.

My favorite aspects of the throwing sling are its light weight, its compact size when rolled up, its pure simplicity, and how quickly, easily, and cheaply it can be fabricated.

Its biggest disadvantage no doubt is the amount of practice it usually requires to gain any degree of proficiency with

Throwing sling rolled up for storing in the kit.

it. I would compare the skill set requirements to those of knife throwing, or possibly even atlatl or spear throwing, in the sense that all of them involve some technique for manually launching projectiles. I prefer the simple overhand, single-hurl launch technique, closely simulating the action of the medieval trebuchet, but you could also try to master the rotating-around-the-head method. For a more detailed study of this weapon, Paladin Press offers a wonderfully informative little book, *The Sling for Sport and Survival*, by Cliff Savage.

A SPEARHEAD FOR THE POOR MAN'S SURVIVAL KIT

A sharply pointed piece of flat steel that can be lashed to a long, sturdy stick in a hurry could save your life in the wild when more efficient weapons may not be with you. In my view, the spearhead, at least for some medium and large survival kits, could be a worthwhile item, especially for the survivor

This spearhead was made from 3/16-inch mild steel plate.

A flat area chiseled on the end of a sturdy stick to accept the spearhead.

The spearhead lashed to the stick with leather cord.

without a firearm who may be forced to greet a large, feral dog or mountain lion. A spearhead is fast and easy to attach to a long stick, and with a heavy spear in hand, the survivor is less likely to be on the menu of those larger creatures in the wild that sport claws and fangs.

I have fabricated spearheads from 3/16-inch flat mild steel plate using only a hacksaw and my bench grinder, although any durable strap of metal (or potentially some other hard and rigid material) could be shaped into a lethal spearhead. The spearhead itself might also serve as a digging trowel or expedient dagger-style knife capable of slicing through rope, prying tree bark apart to access the sap, or harvesting tree branches, depending on the material composition, size, and design of its cutting edge.

To make a quickie spear in a survival situation, file or whittle the end of a long pole or stick of hardwood flat along one side to better mate with the tang of the spearhead. Firmly attach the head to the spear shaft with tight wrappings of cord, wire, or strips of rawhide.

CHAPTER TEN

HOW MUCH SURVIVAL GEAR WOULD A POOR MAN CARRY, ANYWAY?

The stereotypical poor man wilderness traveler tends to be a minimalist. In other words, he doesn't load himself down with too much of the latest, most expensive gear. Most or all of what he does carry he has, more likely than not, used extensively over time, and he knows how to use it effectively. He tends to rely more on his own skills and special knowledge concerning his outdoor lifestyle than on the capabilities of his equipment. This is usually by necessity, because by definition he cannot afford a lot of special gear.

We can easily see how this could apply to a streamlined, self-sufficient form of wilderness survival. The individual who knows how and where to find and acquire food in nature won't need to bring as much food with him on his trips to the wild. The individual who is proficient with the technique of making fire by friction will not feel pressured into buying a $7 magnesium fire starter or a supply of cigarette lighters. The individual who knows how to sew and repair his clothing will not rely on as many spare articles of clothing. The individual who knows how to construct a decent lean-to shelter will not require a tent, and so on.

A blanket, heavy-duty stainless kitchen knife, small ax, BIC lighter, and a plastic water bottle round out this minimalist kit. It provides enough basic provisions to survive in the woods for a total investment of under $10.

I have long had a tendency to carry way more gear into the wild places than I know I really need, and often this creates a burden for me when it comes to my general mobility because the equipment can become surprisingly heavy when there is enough of it. This tendency of mine comes from past experiences when I have found the pressing need for one particular item or another while I'm out of town and simply didn't have it with me when and where I needed it. I guess those experiences have been educational in the sense that I was forced into learning more about how to make do without certain basics—to become more resourceful and self-reliant in many respects—but it also made me think more about planning ahead to prevent those "I forgot to bring it" situations as much as possible.

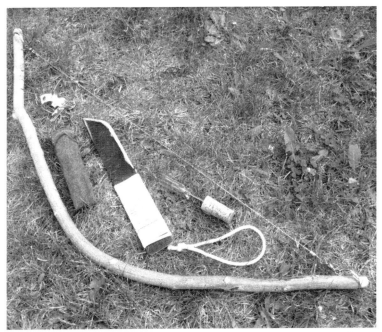

A few examples of truly minimalist tools, including a bow saw fashioned from a wire saw and tree limb, a homemade knife, an awl ground from a screwdriver with its point protected by a wine bottle cork, a cheap can opener, and a simple sewing kit in a small hand-sewn wool bag.

If we divide our gear into two categories—the stuff we regularly use in the outdoors, and the stuff we would keep in an independent specialty kit for outdoor survival purposes only—then we can see the distinction between the type of gear we are focusing more on with this book. We are concerned with compact, lightweight, and in some cases disposable, use-once-and-discard emergency outdoor equipment, as opposed to the regular tent, ax, sheath knife, sleeping bag, and other conventional outdoor gear that always gets used, even though there will always be a fair amount of crossover gear such as small knives and compasses that belong equally to both categories.

The true minimalist will avoid excess and will more often than not go without carrying any sort of separate survival kit

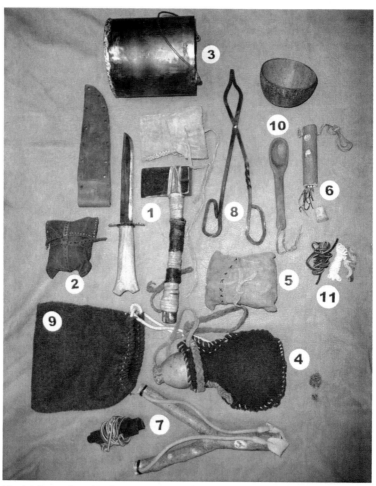

The basic outdoor kit shown in this photo was homemade by the author, as follows: 1) edged tools, including knife made from file and its crudely riveted cowhide sheath, and a homemade hatchet with its own cowhide head cover, 2) flint and steel fire kit in a hand-sewn denim bag, 3) cooking pot made from sheet metal brazed together, 4) gourd canteen in homemade wool canteen cover, 5) homemade sewing kit in hand-stitched buckskin bag, 6) hand-forged fishhooks stored in makeshift wooden capsule, 7) homemade slingshot (using store-bought band in this example), and auxiliary throwing sling rolled up to round out the homemade weapons, 8) hand-forged fire tongs—incredibly handy at the campfire, 9) drawstring bag made from blanket wool, 10) eating utensils, including hand-carved wooden spoon and coconut bowl, and 11) scraps of leather and rawhide lace.

reserved for emergency purposes only. The few items that he will carry will have to serve him day by day, not just in a rare survival emergency.

You can apply this minimalist philosophy in your survival preparations if your equipment priorities are based on common sense, and especially if you have some experience spending time in the woods and already know what you are most likely to need and probably *not* need. You can learn to depend more on your knowledge and skills, which you can always take with you, and less on your physical equipment.

You can even build all of your own outdoor gear from scratch if you want to avoid buying supplies altogether. For a three-day backpacking trip I went on with an old Army buddy into a remote area of Idaho 11 years ago, I decided to construct all of my own equipment as a kind of exercise in self-reliance.

My self-imposed rule was that I had to build everything that I took for my own use, including my backpack, camp

This homemade sewing kit includes a buckskin bag to house everything: small knife made from a hacksaw blade (with a cork blade protector), home-made awl, homemade thimbles, and even homemade sewing needles.

If you're ambitious enough, you could even build your own backpack like this one the author built for a wilderness trip back in August 2001. This is nothing more than a hardwood frame spanned with cowhide webbing, a homemade leather waist belt, and the main pack and shoulder straps hand-sewn from canvas bag material.

tools, fishing tackle, cookware, and even my clothing. We had begun making plans for an August trip in February of that year, so I had six months within which to devise my complete kit.

This was a fun project for me and an educational exercise. The gear I assembled for that trip performed much better overall than I had anticipated. It also reinforced in my mind the awareness that we really don't need as much gear as we usually think we do for our survival in the wild, certainly not the latest and best equipment on the market. With just a few basic handy items, we can fare quite well once we learn whatever we need to know in order to accomplish our goals.

CHAPTER ELEVEN

A FEW EXAMPLES OF INEXPENSIVE BUT FUNCTIONAL WILDERNESS SURVIVAL KITS

Throughout the previous chapters, we have explored the various categories of wilderness survival gear, but at this point the challenge for us is to figure out how to organize all this stuff and make it fit into some sort of compact, self-contained kit. In the photo on the following page, we see an assortment of small survival gear items that will fit into an Altoids tin that measures 2 3/8 inches wide by 3 3/4 inches long by 1 inch thick. Now let's take a look at a few examples of how we might combine some of the same gear plus a few more items to build a more complete, though still fairly compact, pocket-sized kit.

From the accompanying photo, you get a basic idea of what a lot of hunters and backpackers tend to stow in their small kits. The items included are mostly no-nonsense, get-the-job-done-in-an-emergency type of gear in (ideally) the smallest versions possible for a compact kit. The items in this photo address the survival fundamentals, and none of them are prohibitively expensive. That Case XX 2157 SS folding knife (item #1 in the photo), for example, was purchased used at a yard sale for just $2. All ten items

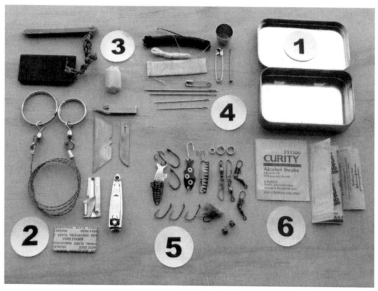

A very compact survival kit that will fit into an Altoids container: 1) Altoids tin, 2) small survival tools, including a wire saw, single-edge razor blade in paper wrapper, P-38 can opener, fingernail clippers, small knife blades, and tweezers, 3) fire-making tools, including ferrocerium striker set in a cedar block that could be whittled into tinder shavings, plus its steel scraper, and tinder ball wrapped in paper, 4) sewing supplies, including assorted needles, thread and dental floss, thimble, safety pins, and a small nail to serve as an expedient awl, 5) miscellaneous small fishing tackle, and 6) first-aid supplies, including bandages, butterfly closures, and an alcohol wipe.

shown will fit into a small pouch that can be carried in the pocket of an army field jacket.

If you choose not to spend any money at all on your outdoor gear, you could still put together a completely functional, very useful survival kit. But you may have to get a bit more creative, as we considered in the previous chapter, if you don't happen to be especially lucky finding a reliable source for free supplies.

Even if you're willing to spend some money to assemble a more comprehensive survival kit than what any serious minimalist would dare even consider, you can nevertheless find ways to keep your costs to a minimum by buying most of the

Here are just some of the most common types of pocket survival kit items: 1) small folding knife, 2) fire-making gear, including cigarette lighter, tinder balls, and that same ferrocerium sparker shown with the Altoids kit, 3) miscellaneous cord, thread, floss, and fish line, 4) coiled wire saw, 5) minimal fishing tackle, 6) signal mirror, 7) folded sheet of aluminum foil for cooking, reflecting, etc., 8) button compass, 9) tweezers, and 10) a space blanket.

items secondhand. An excellent wilderness kit that fits into a large fanny pack and includes mostly used but serviceable equipment is shown in the accompanying photo with the equipment identified and described.

A POOR MAN'S SURVIVAL KIT FROM HOUSEHOLD ITEMS

You can fabricate or prepare a considerable amount of equipment yourself using only the materials you already have around the house. Items assembled from what we already have on hand technically won't be free since they were originally purchased from a store, but they will not require any additional investment. Let's explore a few ideas along these lines.

Here is an example of an ultra-low-budget kit that addresses most of the basics. It includes things for fire making and sewing/clothing repair; improvised weapons; aluminum foil for cooking; cloth rags; coat hanger wire for makeshift bails, handles, and hooks; assorted small tools; plastic trash bag to shed rain or block wind; small diameter rope; and small coffee can, all of which will comfortably fit inside the large coffee can with a lid—and we've already seen how that can be made into a small wood stove.

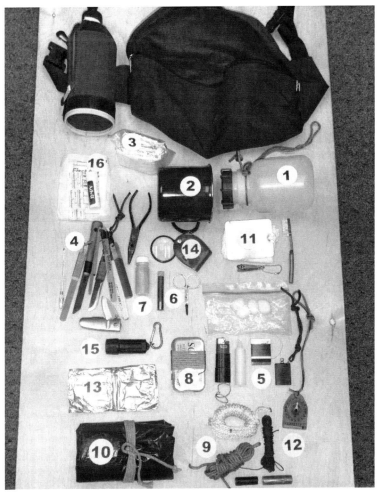

Large fanny pack adventure kit includes 1) plastic drinking bottle, 2) metal cup, 3) Space brand emergency bag (this item was purchased new), 4) small tools, including saw blades, file, homemade knife, needle-nose pliers, tweezers, and small lock-blade knife, 5) fire kit, including lighter, candle, book matches, sparking tool, and cotton balls for tinder, 6) sewing kit, including needles and thread inside a 410 shell, plus tiny scissors, 7) fishing gear in small plastic bottle, 8) the miniature survival kit in Altoids tin we examined earlier, 9) assorted lengths of small rope and cord, 10) 42-gallon 3-mil trash bag for a rain tarp, 11) hygiene items, including mirror, handkerchief, toothbrush, and fingernail clippers, 12) small compass with thermometer, 13) aluminum foil, 14) magnifying glass, 15) small flashlight, and 16) first-aid supplies.

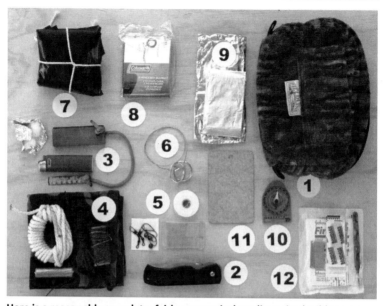

Here is a reasonably complete, fairly economical medium-sized wilderness survival kit: 1) convenient belt pouch kit container that houses all the items shown, 2) lock-blade folding knife with partially serrated edge, 3) fire tools, including disposable lighter, magnesium block, and cotton balls kept in foil, 4) several sizes of small cord and rope, plus rolled strip of duct tape on a handkerchief, 5) basic fishing tackle, including fishhooks, swivels, split-shot sinkers, monofilament fishing line wound on piece of clear hard plastic, and dental floss for additional emergency fish line, 6) coiled wire saw, 7) 33-gallon plastic trash bag, 8) reflective emergency blanket, 9) one foil pan and one folded sheet of aluminum foil, 10) small compass with built-in thermometer, 11) super lightweight and cheap plastic mirror, showing its unreflective backside, and 12) basic first-aid supplies, including bandages, single-edged razor blade, alcohol wipe in foil wrapper, and stainless-steel tweezers.

In the typical kitchen pantry, you would find some ziplock plastic sandwich or freezer bags. In the bathroom medicine cabinet, there may be a bag of cotton balls and a small jar of petroleum jelly. Alternatively, you might collect the lint from the clothes dryer in the laundry room. With just these items, you have everything you need for the ideal wilderness tinder supply to keep in the fire-making kit.

Before leaving the bathroom, you don't want to forget the

Showing the same belt pouch survival kit packed and riding on a belt, with a canteen full of water.

Common household items like plastic bags, tin cans, kitchen knives, matches, cotton balls, bandages, duct tape, string, saw blades, dishrags, and foil can supply the materials we need to create valuable wilderness kits.

dental floss that you already know could serve as fish line, sewing thread, emergency bowstring stands, lightweight snare cord, and, of course, dental floss. Also before leaving the bathroom, you may wish to raid the medicine cabinet once again, this time for some bandages, butterfly sutures, alcohol wipes in sealed foil pouches, and an extra pair of tweezers to appropriate for your kit. There's the bare-bones start of the first-aid portion of your emergency survival kit.

Again back to the pantry, you would likely find a roll of aluminum foil. Tear off a sheet and fold it over itself several times until you have a small square for your kit, to be used as

Boiling water over a coffee can stove in a bowl improvised from a doubled sheet of aluminum foil.

an expedient container, reflector material, or an improvised cooking vessel as we considered previously.

In the garage, you might find a spare or worn-out hacksaw blade. Shorten its length by bending a section back and forth until it breaks, smooth up the resulting sharp edges of the broken end with a file or coarse sandpaper, and then wrap duct tape or cord over several inches of one end to cover the teeth and create a comfortable grip handle. That saw blade could come in handy in the woods when you need to harvest tree branches or cut notches into pieces of wood for various purposes (making bows and arrows, for example). For field use, I prefer the blades with 18 teeth per inch because they cut more aggressively (and faster) through wood than 24 or 32 TPI blades.

You might also find a roll of duct tape in the garage. Tear

A shortened section of a thin hacksaw blade is very narrow and lightweight, inexpensive, will fit into a small kit, and possesses considerable utilitarian value.

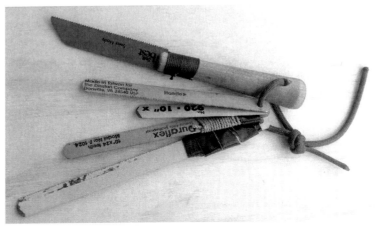

This expedient tool kit comprises assorted saw blades on a cord.

My favorite brand of duct tape is the amazingly sticky and durable Gorilla Tape. The small 1-inch-wide roll shown here is a handy size for toolboxes and survival kits and costs only about $3.

off a few strips and roll them up for storage in your kit; that way they'll be ready when needed to patch holes in tarps, repair clothing, or cover wounds to stop the bleeding in the absence of regular bandages. While in the garage or laundry room, also keep an eye open for small rope or cord, such as a clothesline, garden twine, extra shoelaces, or speaker wire.

Next we venture into the wife's sewing room (with her permission, of course!) and commandeer a spool of heavy-duty sewing thread and some large, sturdy sewing needles with which to assemble a very basic wilderness sewing kit. Your ability to repair clothing, blankets, bags, and other soft equipment could be very important in remote places.

Wherever you keep your fishing tackle merits a visit. From the tackle box you might as well confiscate a half dozen or

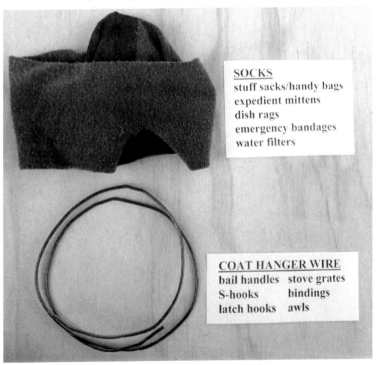

SOCKS
stuff sacks/handy bags
expedient mittens
dish rags
emergency bandages
water filters

COAT HANGER WIRE
bail handles   stove grates
S-hooks   bindings
latch hooks   awls

Common things we expect to find in every home, like socks or coat hangers, could provide us with valuable gear for our poor man's survival kits.

more #6 barbed fishhooks, maybe the same quantity of small split-shot sinkers, some swivels, a few flies and spinning lures, and some monofilament fishing line if you can find a small enough spool to fit into your kit, although the dental floss we already grabbed could serve that application if necessary.

Somewhere in the kitchen you will probably find matches and, if there are any smokers in the house, maybe an extra butane lighter or two. Also in the kitchen you are likely to find some dishrags. Few things in this world have more potential uses than an ordinary rag, especially in the wild where we may need to grab the hot handles of cook pots at the campfire, wipe sweat off our foreheads in the heat of the day, filter dirty water, bandage our cuts, wipe our runny noses in a cold wind, clean our rifle after a day of target practice, mop up unpleasant messes, use as a substitute for toilet paper in a pinch, wipe the dipstick of our vehicle's engine while checking the oil level before driving home from the campsite, and so on.

This little tour of our homes that we have just made reminds us that we can assemble a very usable wilderness kit just from what we find around the house, without having to spend any money whatsoever at the stores.

A COMPLETE KIT CONSISTING OF EVERYTHING NEW FOR UNDER $10!

I discovered that it is indeed possible to assemble a basic wilderness survival kit for less than $10, buying everything new at the stores. Here's how I did it . . .

First, I started with the container to house all the items in the kit. For that I decided on the mess kit idea as we discussed in chapter 1, since it is metal and would provide good protection for the contents, as well as being usable as a cooking vessel. I purchased the cheapest imported aluminum backpacker's mess kit I could find at the local sporting goods store for $1.99.

Next on the shopping list was the cutting tool, and as

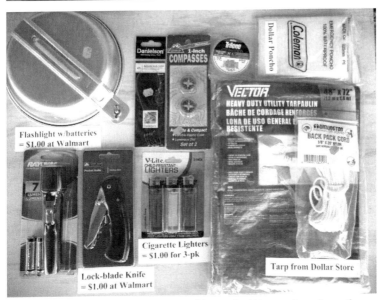

Everything needed to assemble one usable survival kit, purchased new for under $10.

shown in chapter 2, Walmart sells a usable folding lock-blade knife for $1. Also at Walmart I found a small flashlight that came with two AA batteries for a buck. Being able to see in the dark could make a difference to one's survival in the wilderness, if you needed to find your weapons in a hurry in the middle of the night, for example.

At the local Dollar Store I found a lightweight 4- x 6-foot tarpaulin for an emergency shelter, and at the same store I picked up that three-pack of cigarette lighters for a dollar we talked about earlier. I have never been overly impressed with the mostly imported products I've seen for sale in these popular Dollar Stores, but every once in a while you'll find something usable there, and you sure can't beat the price.

At the same sporting goods store where I bought the mess kit I also bought one package of six #6 barbed fishhooks with leader line attached for 39¢, a two-pack of button compasses for 98¢ (and we will only need one for this kit), a 20-yard spool of 6-lb. test nylon fishing line for 98¢, and a 20-foot length of 1/8-inch diameter, braided nylon backpack cord for 50¢. I don't remember exactly where I bought the 99¢ disposable rain poncho seen in the photo, but it's still new in its package.

The total cost for the items just listed (not counting sales tax) was $9.83, and this kit, although admittedly minimal, could conceivably save your life in the wilderness with its rain poncho, tarp, and cord shelter components, butane lighter for making fires, compass for direction orienteering, and fishing line and hooks for harvesting fish for the cooking vessel. And even if I take into consideration the possibility

Survival gear arranged to fit inside the mess kit.

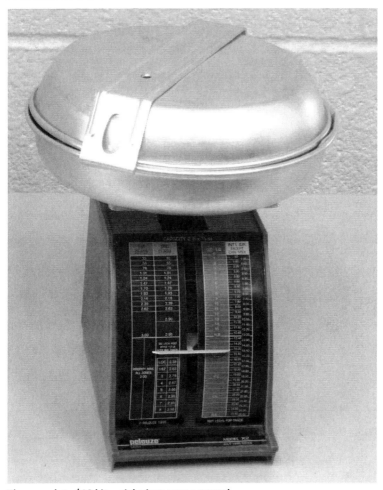

The complete $10 kit weighs just over a pound.

that the batteries in the flashlight might be completely dead by the time I need it, that the small tarp could be a bit *too* small to provide me with adequate cover during a heavy rain, or that the 20 feet of pack cord may not be of sufficient length for its application under certain conditions, the compass should still help me determine direction, at least one of the six fishhooks ought to help me land a fish from a mountain stream or lake, and if all else fails, that knife could surely come in handy when I need to cut through rope or other cord, shape pieces of wood when building weapons and traps, or gut and skin animals. The amount I spent on this whole kit won't even get you three gallons of gasoline at current prices!

The challenge with this $10 kit was to get everything to fit inside that small aluminum mess kit. I wasn't completely sure that everything would fit, but after separating the components from their packaging, folding the tarp as tightly as possible, and only including one of the three lighters and one of the two button compasses, I did finally manage to make everything fit inside the pan and latch the lid closed to hold the whole kit securely together. My biggest concern with this container system is that it is not watertight. However, it does hold the contents firmly together and prevents them from rattling around inside, while also providing a convenient cooking vessel.

A CLOSER LOOK AT THE MOST COMMONLY INCLUDED SURVIVAL KIT ITEMS

Certain popular components of survival gear typically find a place in almost every wilderness kit, whether we are talking specifically about a poor man's kit or more generically about any kind of outdoor survival kit. So let's talk about some of these items that fit our needs for both utility and low cost.

Wire Saw

One of the most useful pieces of survival equipment, and something that is typically stored in even the smallest survival kits, is the popular wire saw. This lightweight device can be coiled up into a compact unit to fit into a very small space, and when stretched out it becomes a perfectly usable saw blade for cutting materials like wood, bone, and plastic.

The wire saw can be used simply by hooking your thumbs into the rings at both ends and spanning the wire taut with both hands for sawing. Just be mindful not to

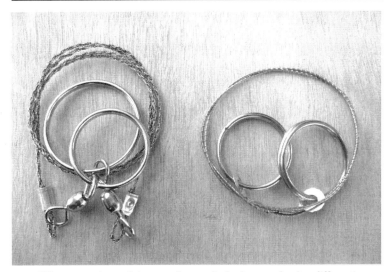

Two different versions of the popular survival wire saw, having different teeth designs. The product on the left was made in England and cost $8. The saw on the right was imported from China and cost under $2. I discovered that either product functions as advertised.

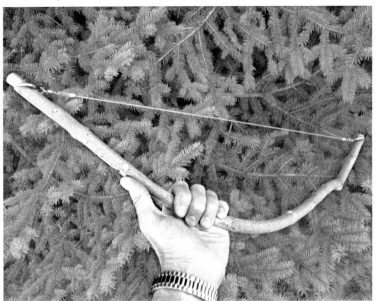

The expedient bow saw made from a tree limb that uses a wire saw for a blade.

Using the wire saw/bow saw to saw through a thick branch.

stretch it too forcefully while sawing or the connection between the ring and blade can break, especially on cheaper models. If that happens to you, don't throw the saw aside in frustration—wrap the exposed end of the blade around a stick a few times to form a T handle and keep sawing.

Alternatively, you can devise a bow saw by carving notches at each end of a flexible tree limb and bending it to accept the rings at each end of the blade. I learned that this works quite well, and it is easy to saw through tree branches up to several inches in diameter with several different versions of the wire saw.

Survival Kit Compasses

Navigation is an important task in the wilderness that we haven't focused on a great deal up to this point, but we should discuss the topic. Nowadays it seems like most serious outdoorsmen rely quite a bit on GPS receivers whenever venturing into the woods, and that might be practical when the latest, most expensive gear is available to us. But remember that in this book, we are assuming we cannot afford high-tech

Three varieties of inexpensive button compasses.

equipment. For us, the old-fashioned magnetic compass needle will have to keep us oriented.

The button compasses available from a number of sources are well suited for our wilderness survival kits because they are ridiculously lightweight, tiny by practically every comparison, and almost always very cheap. In my observation, these products tend to cost under $5, the cheapest costing usually $1 or less (remember that I bought a package of two for 98¢). The arrows of all the button compasses I have seen will point north when the compass is positioned on a level surface and when no iron or steel objects are close enough to interfere with the magnetic field. I cannot envision many reasons why you wouldn't want to keep at least one of these in each of your wilderness survival kits, given their economy of size, weight, and price.

Many readers will be familiar with the makeshift compass trick that involves magnetizing a sewing needle and floating it one way or another on water to obtain a north-south alignment. This allows you the possibility of having a functional compass in your kit without having to sacrifice the space that a regular compass would otherwise occupy. A sewing needle of any conventional size takes up very little space; thus, the sewing needle compass is a viable system for those really compact survival kits that fit into Altoids tins and similar small containers.

Magnetized sewing needle floating on a leaf in a bowl of water formed from aluminum foil. Note that the needle's eye in this case is pointing north.

To create the makeshift compass, simply drag a powerful permanent magnet (as opposed to an electromagnet) along the entire length of a steel sewing needle a dozen or more times, being careful to drag the magnet always in the same direction. The direction you sweep the magnet along the needle will be the end that points *south* in the completed compass. The accompanying photo shows that I swept the magnet toward the point end of the needle, because you can see that the eye is the end that points north, confirmed by a regular compass.

Emergency Blankets

The term "emergency blanket" is commonly applied to any of a variety of blanket-like products intended to help insulate the body from cold and damp conditions. In the army we were issued the lightweight, mostly nylon poncho liners that were considerably less bulky than traditional wool blankets of roughly the same dimensions, and those liners were also a lot lighter in weight. While the poncho liner does not have the same insulating properties as pure virgin wool, it

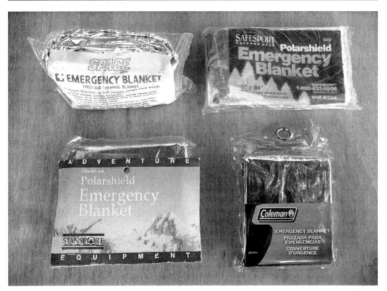

Four different brands of small emergency blankets. Each costs less than $10.

nevertheless makes a huge difference to a soldier on perimeter guard in the cold night air, and it doesn't weigh him down excessively the way a wool blanket would.

Super lightweight thermal blankets are very popular with backpackers because of their economy of weight, unique reflective properties, and low cost. The famous "space blanket" that is sold in every outdoor supply store and consists of plastic film with a silvery or gold-colored reflective surface was originally developed for the American space program in the 1960s. These are also referred to as Mylar blankets, emergency blankets, and thermal blankets.

The standard size of an unfolded emergency blanket is 54 inches by 84 inches, and it weighs about three ounces. Its intended function is mainly to reflect a person's body heat back to him. I think it is particularly interesting to note here that (according to Wikipedia) space blankets have been used by the Taliban to hide their heat signature.

I have never had to resort to using this type of product in

an actual emergency situation, and it's difficult to have much confidence in the effectiveness of something so light and thin, but I do keep one or two in my medium-size survival kits mainly as a supplemental sheltering device simply because I don't know of anything else quite as compact or inexpensive to fill its unique niche.

Emergency Signaling

Nearly every wilderness survival kit you will ever read about in survival books will contain devices for signaling. Mirrors and whistles are the most common, being compact, lightweight, and very effective for their purpose. Fortunately for us, these items are not very expensive.

A little flat pocket mirror, either of metal, glass, or plastic, can be useful to you other than as a signaling tool, as it can help you find something stuck in your eye or help you see around a corner or barrier without exposing your position to possible danger. Any shiny metal can lid or other reflector might help you flash a signal to rescuers over a great distance.

A whistle could also be valuable to you in emergency circumstances when you must get someone's attention and your voice may be difficult to use in a weakened condition or more difficult to hear than the high pitch sound of the whistle. Some people think tough plastic whistles are better than typical metal whistles in cold environments because they won't stick to your lips or tongue when the temperatures dip really low. Others think that is a myth, or the problem could be mitigated by keeping the whistle on a cord around your neck and close to your body to keep it warm. You decide what's best for you.

Bright sounding and surprisingly loud flute-type wooden whistles are not extremely difficult to make. Simply drill a hole through a 2-inch piece of wooden dowel lengthwise, cut a notch into one side, sand a flat surface along one side of a smaller dowel, and fit it firmly into the bigger dowel's hole, and you've got a whistle.

In my experimentation with these things, I have learned that a considerable amount of adjustment is required when

Here is a homemade hardwood whistle that can be carried on a lanyard.

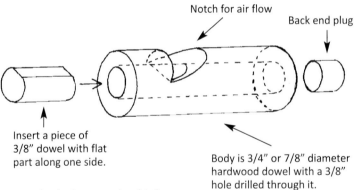

Notch for air flow

Back end plug

Insert a piece of 3/8" dowel with flat part along one side.

Body is 3/4" or 7/8" diameter hardwood dowel with a 3/8" hole drilled through it.

How to make the homemade whistle.

inserting the smaller dowel. I leave a section protruding from the body of the whistle that I can grab with pliers to make adjustments until I get it to sound loudly before sawing it off flush with the mouthpiece end. If the smaller dowel is pushed in too deep, the whistle won't work. If it is not pushed in deep enough, the whistle won't work. If the flat section isn't turned just so in relation to the open notch in the side of the whistle body, or if it is not of the proper dimensions, the whistle won't work, or at least not as well as it should. Also, for this type of whistle to work, the end of the large dowel opposite the mouthpiece end must be plugged with something like a short piece of the small dowel, or you have to block the opening with your finger while blowing. I destroyed my first three sections of hardwood dowel before I finally got a working model.

CHAPTER TWELVE

ADDITIONAL POOR MAN'S SURVIVAL KIT TOOLS

So far we've focused our attention on popular high-priority survival items like knives and fire-making tools, but here we will take a look at some of the smaller handy tools that are commonly overlooked in this context but are nevertheless potentially very utilitarian.

PLIERS

When you need a pair of pliers for a particular task, often no other tool can adequately substitute for it. Pliers are perfect for gripping and pulling various things that are difficult or impossible to get a grip on otherwise.

I find myself reaching for a pair of pliers to manage various tasks quite often, and not just while I'm around the house but also out in the woods. A pair of pliers is indispensable when a rusty nail needs to be pulled out of a fence board, the lid on a small jar is too tight to budge with the grip of the hands alone, a piece of sheet metal needs to be bent a certain way, heavy-gauge wire needs to be twisted or bent, the boiling water in a metal can needs to be poured into a coffee cup, or

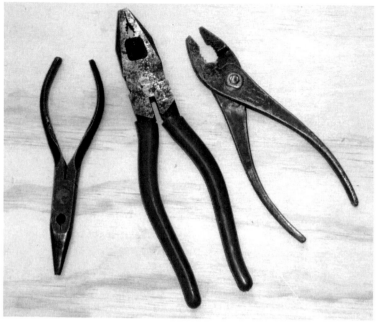

Three used pairs of pliers from yard sales: needle-nose, lineman's, and slip-joint.

a nut on a bolt needs to be turned when the proper fitting wrench is not available.

It is true that a pair of pliers will add weight and bulk to any field kit, and there is really no end to the different types of tools we would like to have with us in remote places, but the utility value of these devices definitely makes them worth considering for our kit. Pliers are commonly found at yard sales, typically for 50¢ or a dollar a pair. I like slip-joint pliers because their jaws can be adjusted for gripping larger items like small jar lids, but I also like needle-nose pliers for gripping things within narrow spaces.

The multifunction plier tools that hit the market with a splash close to 30 years ago are even more popular today, and they are available in a wide variety of configurations and under various brand names, the most common being Leatherman, Gerber, SOG, Schrade, and Buck Knives. My personal

Pliers-type multitools: imported American Camper multitool on the left, and the higher quality—and much more expensive—Leatherman Super Tool at right.

favorites are the Leatherman Super Tool and the Leatherman Wave Tool. These products contain a wonderful assortment of handy small tools like the needle-nose pliers, locking knife blades, saw blades, files, screwdrivers, and can openers. Readers will notice that I have used my well-worn Super Tool frequently with the projects described throughout this book.

I could go on and on about how useful I find this type of tool, but the best of them, costing anywhere from close to $50 on up to $80 or more, are not exactly priced for the poor man. And I do not remember ever seeing any good condition, brand-name multitools at yard sales or secondhand stores at giveaway prices (a testament to their popularity), so I think we're pretty much stuck with those new retail prices when planning our budget allowances.

If the higher price of a first-rate multitool puts you off, there are those cheap imitations on the market to consider.

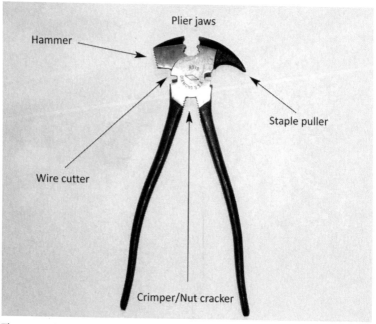

The versatile fence pliers "multitool."

Some of the tools they feature are actually usable in my experience, plus the whole combination typically costs less than $10. I have never been a huge fan of tools imported from Taiwan or China, but I don't think we should necessarily rule them out for our purpose here.

Another pliers tool that I believe merits our attention is the traditional fence pliers, so called because its special features are well suited to performing repairs on fences. It has a horn for hooking under and prying large staples and a hammer face for driving nails or staples into fence boards.

Because it is capable of performing several tasks besides merely gripping, it is a true multifunction or combination tool, in my view. It is not the lightest hand tool you will ever find for your backpack, but when you need a long-handled pair of pliers, a hammer, a staple puller, or a heavy wire cutter, you'll have them with the fence pliers. Prices vary depending on brand and retailer, but a new pair will normally run $10 and up, while you should never have to pay more than $2 or $3 for a used pair in good condition at a yard sale.

SWISS ARMY KNIVES

The genuine Swiss Army knives (i.e., those made in Switzerland) are famous for their compactness and their amazingly versatile utility value, with all of their popular little tools, but they are not exactly cheap. The two brand names of high-quality Swiss Army knives that come in a wide array of models are Wenger and Victorinox.

One can find cheap imitations imported from countries like China and, when picked up used at sales, generally cost less than a dollar. For that price, a poor man could surely make use of some of the blades. I found that the scissors on a

My son purchased this imported imitation of a Swiss Army knife at a yard sale for 50¢.

used Chinese-made Swiss Army knife copy will cut cardboard and paper every bit as well as will the scissors on my much more expensive Victorinox model. So this is something to consider for a poor man's kit.

NAIL CLIPPERS

Some readers will undoubtedly not agree with me that fingernail clippers merit inclusion in the small- to medium-sized wilderness survival kits, but I usually tend to include this tool.

First of all, I find myself using the clippers quite often because my fingernails seem to grow fast and I prefer keeping my nails pretty short to prevent snagging on clothing or scratching my eyes, as well as to minimize the dirt-under-the-fingernails annoyance. I realize that I could keep my nails short using other tools like scissors or files, but the little clippers just handle that job so much easier. So, in this application the fingernail clippers belong in the personal hygiene category, which I consider an important survival fundamental (though maybe more for the long term than the short term).

Second, the little tool is very handy for other purposes. I

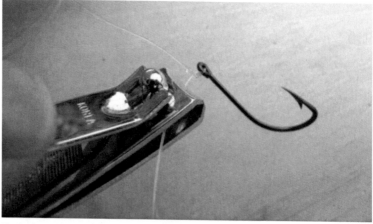

Typical stainless steel fingernail clippers being used to trim excess fish line at the knot securing the fishhook.

have used them for cutting and trimming fishing line and for clipping the weed whacker cord when necessary while trimming my yard. Using clippers with only one hand can be more convenient than trying to cut small line with the blade of a knife, which usually takes two—one to hold the knife and the other to hold the cord. The most common style of clippers also includes a small nail file, which could potentially be used in shaping small objects of other materials like wood or bone. So, in this sense the fingernail clippers could be thought of as a type of multitool. As is true with scissors, fingernail clippers are not a direct lifesaving piece of equipment, but they can sure make a difference to your quality of life in the wilderness.

Finally, the item is very small, lightweight, and best of all, cheap! In my view, this is one of the niftiest little tools ever invented.

A HOMEMADE MULTIFUNCTION
TOOL FOR THE WILDERNESS

I recently modified a well-used flat bastard file to create a pot handle for around the campfire, and what I

This bastard file has been modified to serve multiple wilderness survival purposes.

ultimately ended up with was in fact a handy multipurpose tool for the wilderness.

The file I started with lacked a handle, so I notched both edges of its tang with a row of short hacksaw cuts to prepare it for attachment to a conventional wooden file handle. I would be using epoxy (J.B. Weld, in this case) to hold the handle on permanently, and the notches do help the glue interlock with the tang and handle for a more secure connection.

Before adding the handle, I heated the tip end of the file in my forge and bent a short section of it into an L-shape so that its tip would slide under the bracket mounted on the side of a mess kit pot. If you don't have access to a blacksmith forge, the tip can be heated for bending using an acetylene torch or even in a woodstove or fireplace. In its annealed state after being heated in the forge and slowly cooled, I was able to easily grind and saw various notches into the file that would help make it into a multipurpose tool.

Before adding the handle, I retempered the file so that it

Using the makeshift tool as a mess kit pot handle.

One edge of the tool was ground smooth to facilitate flint scraping, shown here with a piece of flint.

would create sparks if scraped against a piece of sharp flint, and I ground the teeth off the edge on one side for this purpose. So now this tool will also serve, in conjunction with a piece of sharp flint, as a fire starter.

I drilled a 7/16-inch diameter hole through the handle to accept a lanyard cord with which to tether or hang the tool, and this hole is also large enough to facilitate using the tool as a wrench to straighten kinks out of expedient arrow shafts in a survival situation.

This makeshift tool is very versatile, as it can be used to lift a pail or bucket by its bail using its notch on one edge, form a handle on a mess kit pot that features the common bracket this type of handle will fit, as a nail puller claw (although the hard file steel is relatively brittle and could possibly snap under heavy leverage stress), or in conjunction with flint to make fire as described above. And with its claw-shaped end, I discovered that it works as a decent back-scratcher.

Old, dirty, dull, or chipped files are commonly offered at garage sales for less than a dollar apiece, so this type of makeshift multitool is truly a viable option for just about any creative poor man.

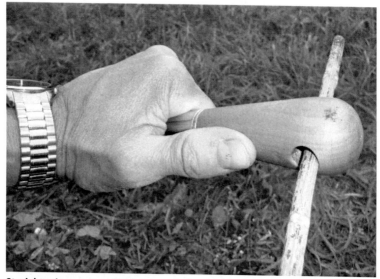

Straightening an expedient arrow shaft using the lanyard hole in the makeshift tool's handle.

Using the notch in the tip to pull a nail out of a board.

Lifting a bucket by its bail.

SMALL FILES FOR THE SURVIVAL KIT

We've just observed how we can modify a file for other purposes, but we may also wish to keep one in our kit just to use as a file. Files are incredibly versatile tools that can be used for sharpening blades or other tools, smoothing up sharp or jagged edges of metal to make things safer, shaping objects out of wood, bone, plastic, metal, or horn, and all

A typical inexpensive and compact fishhook file.

sorts of other tasks. The tiny metal files sold in fishing tackle stores and bait shops for sharpening fishhooks are very light and compact and not at all expensive. Three dollars or less will buy you a very small metal file that might be just perfect for your kit.

To make a fishhook file even more compact and suitable for stowing in a small survival kit, heat the tang with a propane torch and, using needle-nosed pliers, roll the narrow tang into an eye for attaching a cord.

SMALL CLAMPS

Certain chores involving sewing, fly tying, mending fishing tackle, keeping once-opened food pouches closed, or gluing small things together can often be much easier to accomplish with the help of small clamping devices because each of us has only two hands and a limited number of fingers. For their utility value, I believe small clamps can be worth adding to a survival kit where space allows.

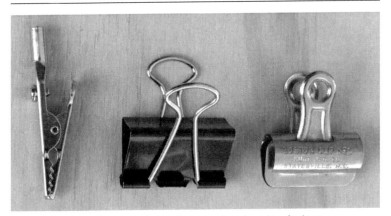

Three examples of very small, very inexpensive clamping devices.

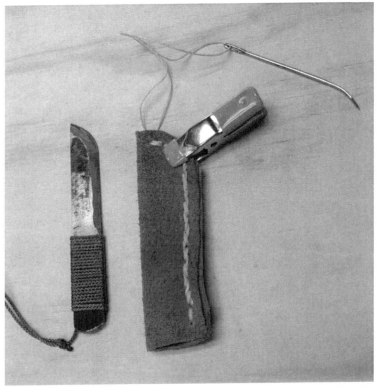

A small clamp holding folds of leather in alignment while you stitch a sheath for a small homemade knife.

Tiny clamps are very inexpensive, available in every store that carries home and office supplies or hardware items, and they weigh almost nothing. Yet they will provide considerable utility value in certain situations.

FINAL THOUGHTS

Throughout this book we have explored various strategies for building personal survival kits on a shoestring budget, as well as modifying and adapting common materials for use in the wilderness. Hopefully the information has been instructive, but at the very least I am confident that reading this book will inspire new and in some instances even better ideas.

Since you have now seen just how some usable outdoor gear can be makeshift or acquired without spending much money, you might as well get busy experimenting with some of these projects and assembling some kits. If you end up with extra kits, you can keep a separate one in each of your automobiles, snowmobiles, ATVs, fishing tackle boxes, saddlebags, or backpacks. If you have any gear left over, use it for practice.

I know you've heard this many times, but in the end, our best survival kit is our brain, because we can generally think our way through most predicaments. And if you take the initiative right now to learn all that you can from as many different sources as you can—learn which kinds of wild plants are edible, how to tie the most versatile knots, how to create and safely control fire, how to build and use primitive weapons and traps, how to administer basic first aid, how to find your way in the wilderness—then you will surely stand a better chance in any survival situation, anywhere in the world.

So that's what I strive to do everyday, to learn more about all of these things. I always become inspired whenever I discover something I didn't previously know, and of course I can hardly wait until the next time I can share it with readers in a new book. Thanks for reading!